COLLECTED
ESSAYS OF
George
Bendall

Mentors of New Thought Series

COLLECTED
ESSAYS OF
George
Bendall

Compiled by Ann Bendall

 DEVORSS *Publications*

ISBN: 0-87516-669-5

Library of Congress Catalog Card No.: 94-70458

Printed in the United States of America

DeVorss & Company, Publishers
Box 550
Marina del Rey, CA 90294-0550

Contents

George Parker Bendall
(1919-1992)

IN THE FALL of 1989 someone in my office mentioned that there was a book of Ernest Holmes' talks newly published —by Dr. George Bendall, the Religious Science minister who had taken up residence with Dr. Holmes upon the passing of Holmes' wife, Hazel, and who had been his close confidant, liaison man, and aide-de-camp until Holmes' passing in 1960.

This was wonderful news, and the more wonderful for also relating that Dr. Bendall lived and had his ministry in nearby Manhattan Beach. I was at once on the telephone to Dr. Bendall, and that Saturday found me driving down No. Aviation Boulevard in Manhattan Beach, looking for the South Bay Church of Religious Science and its minister, whom I found alone in a small suite of rooms the largest of which served as the church "hall."

George Bendall was in every way impressive—tall, ruggedly good-looking, a brilliant metaphysician (as I very soon learned), and a storehouse of intimate knowledge of Ernest Holmes and the Religious Science movement. His personal library was also impressive. Its size alone was arresting, but a close look at some of the old and occasionally obscure titles told me at once that

1

here was a New Thought scholar's resource such as you seldom encounter.

What never escaped the attention for a moment was the presence one sensed of Ernest Holmes. It wasn't just the portrait executed by the beach artist in the course of a stroll the two men took along the shore at Santa Monica more than 30 years earlier —one of the few portraits of himself, by the way, that Ernest Holmes ever liked, and which occupied an icon-like place in Dr. Bendall's modest office. Rather it was that everything, from the other office appointments to the atmosphere in which Dr. Bendall moved, bespoke *Ernest Holmes*. Here, dedication—better, consecration—to the founder of Religious Science definitely held sway.

That day, a friendship was born—one that would find me both Dr. Bendall's student and, later, collaborator in the expansion of his *Holmes Papers* publishing project, the first volume of which had been the occasion of our meeting. These were wonderfully off-the-cuff talks given by Ernest Holmes, many of them privately, in the last years of his life—talks like just about nothing else in print by Holmes or, for that matter, by anyone else.

The Philosophy of Ernest Holmes was the first volume in the series—a collection of rare and diverse pieces, including one of Ernest's poems earmarked for *The Voice Celestial** but "killed" by brother Fenwicke Holmes, despite Ernest's enthusiasm for it. It ended up a treasured keepsake in the possession of Dr. Bendall—along with so many other things passed on to him by his teacher and mentor, the most precious being the hours and hours of "tutorial" that he had in those two years of residence in the Holmes household that I wanted to know all about.

"Knowing all about" those two years, however, would probably have taken George more than the several years we were to have together on this planet for the telling. Countless had been

---

* An epic poem composed by Ernest and Fenwicke Holmes, published in 1960.

the lessons, anecdotes, incidents, gatherings, discussions, break-throughs, decisions, surprises, healings, demonstrations . . . and there had been poignancies, misadventures, disappoint-ments too . . . and the final heartbreak of Ernest Holmes' depar-ture from the scene he had created over a period of more than 40 years for others to come upon and take from—fruits of richer living.

I soon learned that George Bendall had been one of the most avid takers. In Ernest Holmes' Science of Mind he saw the quin-tessence of everything that New Thought had so far found and demonstrated. Here was the clearest, most economically scien-tific statement of the long journeying of an idea from Phineas Parkhurst Quimby's serious beginnings in 1838 to Holmes' refinement of it in his *Science of Mind* textbook's definitive statement of exactly a century later.

I learned that George Bendall's life was a continuous dedi-cation to the memory and legacy of his teacher. As chapter af-ter chapter of it unfolded in conversation, I realized that his had been an extraordinary story from the outset. A Southern ''aris-tocrat'' by birth and an engineering prodigy by nature and train-ing—he was among the few hundred young men personally exempted from military conscription by President Franklin Roosevelt for their value to the home front—he had also found time to organize a group of truth-seekers that met regularly at New York's prestigious Hotel Shelburne. But it was his en-counter with one of Ernest Holmes' books that turned his life around—and westward to Los Angeles in a journey that at first nearly claimed his life in a disaster but that happily issued in his meeting Dr. Holmes and realizing that the seeking part of his *life's* journey was over. In ''Ernest Holmes Remembered'' (pp. 97–132), he tells us about all this and carries the story forward to the extraordinary summons to Ernest Holmes' side upon the sudden death of Holmes' wife, Hazel, in 1957.

By this time, George Bendall had not only joined the Reli-gious Science movement but had been ordained as a minister-at-large. These concluding years of Holmes' life (he passed away in 1960) became the occasion of Bendall's greatest growth as he both served and learned directly from this great religious philosopher. Nor was it all adulation by any means. Holmes didn't want a sycophant for a companion, liaison man, and aide-de-camp; and George, being George, wasn't about to be one anyway. In fact, his memoir of these years is unsparing of the full variety of tints and hues of coloration in which *both* men emerge.

George's situation midway the founder of Religious Science (who was now directing from the sidelines largely through him) and the founder's movement—with its headquarters, churches, officers, ministers, practitioners, and other assorted elements—was often uncomfortable. And when Holmes passed on, he was rudely pushed aside by the power brokers, who saw themselves as the exclusive inheritors of the Holmes mantle. Bendall, whose only "base" was an empty 23-room house that he now had to vacate, was left to shift largely for himself.

One of today's few remaining veterans of the earlier years of Religious Science, who had been closely associated with Ernest Holmes for quite some time before the advent of George Bendall, has told me:

> Ernest was extremely fond of George. Unfortunately, this fondness did not sit well with other personalities in the movement, who were, frankly, jealous of Ernest's partiality to him and also not a little resentful of the "inside track" and privileged position that George enjoyed. Add to that the fact that George was often caught in the middle between Ernest and these other people, and it tells you a lot.

It was at this point that George Bendall determined upon his course. In fact, it was a course largely set by Holmes quite some time before: "Your real gifts are as a teacher," he had told his protégé, "and the entire Religious Science field is your real class-room and pulpit." In his determination to ensure that Holmes' teaching in its integrity, as well as his memory, should be served whatever might be the fortunes of the Religious Science move-ment at the hands of its hierarchs, George decided to take his teacher's commission seriously.

How fortunate for us! With today's hindsight we can appreci-ate how essential this task would prove to be, for the next three decades would see not only the predictably variable fortunes that any religious organization might experience, but a decided drift, in many quarters, from Holmes' teaching—often, of course, in the name of forward motion; but often, too, as the consequence of individual and corporate folly. To borrow one of George Ben-dall's inimitable sayings, "We had gotten to the point where we had not only thrown out the baby with the bath water; we were throwing out the baby's father too."

George, still credentialed and now fortified with an impres-sive L.H.D., next served as minister of the Valley Oaks (Calif.) Church of Religious Science. This was followed by his establish-ment of an independent Religious Science church in Manhattan Beach, which became his base for a five-pronged (but one-man) effort to honor his lifetime commitment to Ernest Holmes: serv-ing a ministry; maintaining a traveling lectureship on the per-son and teaching of his mentor; assuming a teaching position with Ernest Holmes College; standing in for Dr. William Hor-naday on numerous occasions at Founder's Church of Religious Science in Los Angeles; and undertaking the long-term, multi-volume project of publishing Ernest Holmes' later talks, both public and private. This became the unique series known as *The Holmes Papers*, in three volumes,* and into it Dr. Bendall poured thousands of dollars and all of his heart, his principal

---

* Vol. 1: *The Philosophy of Ernest Holmes* (1989); vol. 2: *The Anatomy of Healing Prayer* (1991); and vol. 3: *Ideas of Power* (1992).

recompense being the satisfaction of knowing that unique facets of Ernest Holmes' personality, teaching, and later maturity had at last been made public and—no overstatement—immortalized.

It was during the time of his work on *The Holmes Papers* that Dr. Bendall met up once again with a friend of former years who would now become his wife—Ann. And with Ann would come a strength, stability, and support previously wanting in his life: in a word, *home*—but more than that; for in Ann, George found a staunch collaborator and supporter of his lifework.

After concluding the Manhattan Beach ministry, George began a new one in Salem (Ore.) at Woodland Chapel, along with radio work on the Science of Mind. Always restless, and heedless of his own comfort and convenience, he also welcomed the continuing calls from Dr. Hornaday and Founder's Church, as well as the ministerial and lecture tours he and Ann embarked upon almost regularly.

Upon William Hornaday's passing, in March of 1992—Founder's first and only pastor since its establishment 32 years earlier—Dr. Bendall was called to assume this flagship pulpit of Religious Science. It was entirely fitting that he, by then one of no more than a handful of the remaining Science of Mind "giants"—and just about the last still active—should follow Dr. Hornaday to this position; although the circumstances were anything but propitious, and the new post was in many ways more harrying than gratifying. It can be no coincidence, therefore, that he did not last long in it. Seven months after succeeding him, George Bendall once more followed—and now joined—his friend William Hornaday.

All lives are unique, but George Bendall's was "more unique" than most. His unique knowledge of Ernest Holmes, his unique work in making Holmes' intimate talks public, his unique brand of dedication to his teacher and mentor, and his unique role in the history of Religious Science—all this can obscure something else also most rare, especially today: a brilliant metaphysical mind that dazzled his students (including this writer).

Ernest Holmes was probably right in intuitively grasping at the very outset that George Bendall's greatest gift lay in teaching. The present collection, however, represents the other side of George Bendall's career: the ministry to congregations spanning several decades and a wide geography of pulpits and classrooms. The essays that follow are Dr. Bendall's keen metaphysics translated into the art of living, where the unity of heart, mind, and spirit finds the kind of intense celebration that Dr. Bendall brought to pulpit and classroom alike. And his memoir of his teacher, in whose service he both found and gave his life, is a priceless document that only Ernest Holmes' "beloved disciple" could have written.

Although many a great minister and teacher comes to be forgotten over time, posterity will likely be kinder to George Bendall, owing to the several unconventional and historically significant roles he played within the Religious Science tradition. In addition to personally delivering to us some of its most precious, long-buried materials, he remains as important to a true understanding of the history of his tradition as he was "very important to Ernest Holmes in his last lonely years."* Here, then, we salute his memory with love and gratitude.

Arthur Vergara

* Elaine St. Johns in *Science of Mind* magazine (Dec. 1987), "Light, Love, and Law: The Three Last Gifts of Ernest Holmes," p. 33.

NOTE Footnotes have been added to Dr. Bendall's text for the reader's information.

What It's All About

IN THE STATEMENT OF PRINCIPLES of Religious Science, Ernest Holmes says: We believe in the unity of all life and that the highest God and the innermost God is one God. We believe the universal Spirit, which is God, operates through a universal Mind, which is the Law of God, and that we are surrounded by this creative Mind which receives the direct impress of our thought and acts upon it.

That is what the whole teaching is. There isn't anything else. It's that simple.

Man and God are one and can't be separated. Old theology has for years created a separation where by supplication we have to go to get a special intercessor to bridge between man and God. Ernest couldn't even make sense out of that logically; his basis was *One, One, One.* Man and God are not separate, they are One. And we can understand this when we begin to get into the teaching—when we understand that we couldn't pray for anybody unless within us were the same thing that is in the other individual. It's the whole secret of absent treatment. So we see that the Infinite Intelligent Creative Energy or Source that surrounds us can work for us only by working through us. There-

9

fore our whole system of teaching is to provide an easy channel to sacrifice our self-will and to provide an easy channel for this Energy or Source to operate through us. And Ernest always pointed out that the very conditions that we're complaining about—that we feel we're suffering from—are actually a misuse of the Power, because it works whether we suffer or whether we're happy—because the law of cause and effect has no judgment and works for us every time that we think; and ignorance of it excuses no one from its effects. It is really a law of reflection. It's the same as standing in front of a mirror and clenching your fist: a fist clenches back at you.

An exercise I give is to stand in front of a mirror and say, "I am a living, loving, worthy expression of God." (The first time, you say to yourself "I don't really believe this"; then, along about the second or third week, you will find that your whole facial expression changes: the mirror is reflecting back the conviction of thought.) So the whole system that we're talking about works by a law of reflection—a response that corresponds identically to what we're thinking and feeling.

If you want to put a fancy title on it, it's the reciprocal action between us as individuals and a universal subjectivity, or a universal subconscious, that's picking up the impression and reflecting it back. But you see, we have to remember, with the Law of Mind, as with any other universal law of nature: *it's not personal to any one person. We* personalize it—according to the way we believe it and according to the way we use it. Therefore the Law has a force or energy that responds to the thought that we are having (or to our mental atttitude) by reflecting it back into our life in terms of experience. The idea, then, is that *it's done unto us as we believe.*

The "Eleventh Commandment" of Jesus says, "Love one another as I have loved you"; and when you do, you get that love coming back to you: because we cannot take anybody's love and affection; we only get our own coming back in a circle. Thus, in our being a part of the Mind of God, every emotion that we give out is acted upon and returned to us. So don't be confused about this thing that we call Law. If you want to, pretend that the Law is a mirror and that you're looking at your life in the mirror of your own thoughts and your own feelings. The conditions that surround you, the activity that is surrounding you, the people that surround you—all are a result of your thinking.

When you define something and you say it's a law, it becomes easier to say, "This is the way the thing works." If I take a book and put it *here*, there is a law of gravity that holds it here; and if I take it and move it *there*, the law of gravity is still working, because the law is there. Ernest Holmes always said that what we're trying to do is not to *create* principles but to *find out what they are* and try to harmonize ourselves with those principles. He said that the subconscious mind is the Law of God. It works—but it can only produce what is given to it as material. Cause and effect, sowing and reaping, action and reaction, impression and expression: it can only give back what you put into it. So, as you think, it takes it. You can't take anything out of it; what you put into it is returned to you.

And here's the thing that throws many people: they say, "You mean, God doesn't care for me personally?" because the action of the Law is impersonal; it is no respecter of persons. It doesn't say, "I am going to give Ruth or Joe a better shot when they think, because they are nice people." It doesn't say, "I am not going to give Sam or Doris the best, because they are not nice people." It's totally impersonal in that whatever is placed upon it, it returns to you. If you select a cabbage seed and plant it, you will get back cabbages. The action of the soil doesn't say, "What do they want cabbages for? I think they need roses in the house!" You get cabbages. When you *plant* roses, *then* you get roses back. You get back no matter what it is, even though it may for some reason not be what you *think* you want.

The Law is impersonal, so it doesn't know sick from well.

But the divine pattern within you knows that you are born to be well, born to be whole; and if you deviate from that, you can return to it by accepting that "I am an expression of God, whole, healthy, and complete." *But the Law doesn't know it.* So if you say, "I have to get out of this physical condition," the Law says, "Oh you've got a *condition*?!?" and the more power you give it, the more of it you've got. But if you say, "I accept that I am freed from anything unlike my divine expression as a child of God, and it is my right to be healthy and well," then that's fine. The Law responds to it.

Similarly, the Law doesn't know happy from unhappy. The Law doesn't know that you are unhappy or happy, because that would constitute judgment—and so the action of the Law would not be immutable, and you and I would be like little toy people, wound up and running around for the delight of some Big Something-or-other.

We condition this force—the Law, the subconscious, the subjective, call it what you will—by *deciding* and *repeating* what we want over and over again until finally we believe it to such an extent that we have made a penetration and this creative medium then says: "OK: you've got it and I'll grow it and we'll both walk away with it!" So we condition ourselves. We condition ourselves by recognizing that there is the Spirit of God within us and that this Spirit gives us the power of choice—each one of us individually. And God so loves human life personally that He gives us the right to choose to be well, to choose to be happy, to choose to be abundant—or to be sick, unhappy, or broke. And God's Law doesn't know the difference.

But the Love is there. What greater love could we have than to be given total authority over our own individual life? You see, Jesus' method of healing was very interesting and very simple; he was a very simple teacher and a great example. He would look at a condition of distortion with his conscious eye as you and I would. *We'd* say, "My! Look at how sick this person is!" Jesus would look, but he would see something else. He would see the divine pattern of God within that individual. He would divert attention away from the focus of the condition by any method, because he knew that we as human beings love to worship our suffering.

I don't know where we got this from; God certainly isn't a martyr. It must have been the first caveman that decided he was going to suffer and it's hung around in our genes ever since. But Jesus would divert attention from the focus of the condition by doing something like waving his hand, and then from within he would project that image of total wholeness. And it was done. This was the method that Phineas Parkhurst Quimby, the founder of New Thought, established—separate the belief from the believer. Jesus would lift off the false and see only what was underneath the effect.

Jesus didn't create anything. He revealed what already was there. But the work lay in changing the subconscious thinking of the individual so that the mirror reflection would reflect the inherited perfection. So often we get involved because of the world of experiences that we live in—and we are experience-centered people. We get involved in those experiences to such an extent that we get wrapped in our own destructive thinking and the destructive thinking of the world. And when we do, our affairs mirror and return all this back to us.

I think we have to finally accept—and Ernest Holmes was a great believer in this—that what we call our subconscious is really the Mind of God. Every one of us has used it consciously and unconsciously to bring ourselves to the point where we are in our lives today. The life you live, the life you have experienced, has been that which you have directed to the mirror, and the mirror has reflected it back. But I think that the greatest thing is that this warm, encompassing, loving Energy-Intelligence that we call God imparted Life to us by an act of divine givingness—and gave us the right to use it, express it, enjoy it, and fulfill it, willingly and permissively, employing all of the great creative powers of the Intelligence that we talk about in Science of Mind. When we use these powers for our health, our wholeness, our harmony, and our abundance, we are in a state of grace. When we misdirect them, so that we suffer or hurt, we have fallen from grace.

But you see, we have to keep remembering something that people often forget. They think that in our teaching they're going to use these "creative" powers and actually *create* something—that they are going to *make something happen*. They're going to take matter and they are going to "put" spiritual processes *into* it; they're going to take a spiritual idea and make it materialize in front of their eyes. But that isn't so—because God is the thing they think they've created. You see, even if you create a miserable experience God is still there. Because if there is nothing else but God, then what you label as miserable is what you have decreed—so that's what you experience. But fortunately, out of this whole thing comes a new chance to those of us who decide that we want to establish a new sense of creative energy. What you and I do in this teaching is to redirect a stream of creative energy.

What this gives us the ability to do is *not* to take a miserable, old experience and sit down and say, "I'm going to treat this miserable experience and let rays from the moon come down and transform it." No, that isn't what we're given to do. We're going to withdraw the creative energy from the miserable experience—the energy which established that form—because the principle of creativity is always active—and the creative energy will be redirected to that which is good and harmonious and abundant. The miserable experience is really only an inert something—more nothing than something! I can leave it or I can take it and "move" it. It's that simple in the redirection of the creative energy.

I think Emerson said much the same thing: "There's a place

where everybody can let out the reins." In the streets of old Boston and Cambridge they drove horse-drawn vehicles and had speed limits just as we do; you couldn't let out the reins and let the horses gallop—you had to conform to all the conditions of the city. But when you reached the country roads, you could let the reins out and let the horse gallop and run. So there's a place where everyone can let out his or her reins. The Science of Mind as formulated and established by Dr. Ernest Holmes tells us we have the right to let out the reins without fear. We have a right to use this great thing for the pure fun and enjoyment of it. It's all within us.

You see, we and our relationships and experiences are all a part of the color, the tone, the love, the harmony, and the giving that Spirit has been allowed to reciprocate. You can sum it up very simply with words that have lasted a long time: there's only "one Wisdom to understand the thought by which all things are steered through all things." And hundreds of years before the teachings of Jesus, this from Isaiah: "Surely as I have thought, so shall it come to pass and as I have purposed, so shall it stand."

We're asked many times, "How do you feel about other teachings?" We love them; we honor others' right to believe what they want to believe. After all, we believe what *we* want to believe. But within ourselves we know that there is only one God. And this isn't a denominational God. We also know that we don't support "foxhole prayer"—the on-again, off-again type of prayer that is usually good only under fire; and then before the prayer works, the one praying returns to the state of destructive thinking, because he hasn't continuously honored the belief of a loving, living God.

People say to me: "In your teaching, you people are your own Jesus"; and as I think about it, I consider it a tremendous compliment and something we should work toward—because Jesus said, "My Father within you can do even greater things than these which now I'm doing.'' Whatever the religious terminology used, we know that the ''breaks'' of life can come to any individual who will accept the principles, provide a channel for them to work, have a desire, make a decision, have the determination, and *do it*.

You see, this is perhaps the most difficult thing about our teaching: *We have to work at it*. We don't go and sit down and someone says, ''This is what you do; this is what you can't do.'' ''If you do this you're bad; if you do this, that's good.'' We don't do that. We say to you: you decide and use the principles and the good within your own life, by focusing and dwelling continuously on purposeful, constructive mental and emotional ideas. We have to keep working at it. Without this you *may* get the ''breaks,'' but you won't know what to do with them, because *we make our own luck*.

You see, the whole thing is practice, and the world doesn't know much about that. Ernest Holmes always insisted that the Science of Mind is a teaching *and a practice*. And as much as they say they know, the world doesn't know about our practice; and there are many in New Thought who don't know about the practice either. I think we have a secret that only those of us who really get into the teaching know anything about. You listen to people talk—the doctor, the psychiatrist, the psychologist, the philosopher, the religionist—and they are all good; but they stop at the point where we begin, which is that we believe we are dealing at first hand with a cosmic Creativity, the Ancient of Days, the primordial Substance, the absolute of Law, the availability of an omnipotent Omnipresence, and the use of the inspiration we can receive from It.

People say, ''Your thing is kind of abstract,'' and I answer, ''That may be so to your mind. But if there is only one God and one Source, and God is all, then how could there be anything 'abstract' as distinct from the concrete, the real?'' Because the real must be formed from the invisible, and the invisible then passes into it; so that which is referred to as absolute (or "abstract") is real, because the real itself is absolute, and there can never be any deviation from it.

We believe that once we have generated this energy, we can direct it by the enforcement of our word; but we also know that we don't put any power in it. We know that we release that which is the perfection within. This is the way the teaching was put together. I know that there is a consciousness, an awareness in me, and I know there is a consciousness and awareness within you. But I arrive at it without having to work with contradictions or pairs of opposites and without falling into the trap of serving God or mammon. This is our ideal; this is our secret—the instantaneous availability of an absolutism, if you want to call it that, which doesn't reconcile any opposites, contradictions, or relativities but brings them up into the neutralizing presence and power of One God, One Life, and One Love—carrying everything into a field of unity without division, yet leaving it all very distinct, very clear, and very easily identifiable. There is just as much life in an elephant, a plant, a flea, and a whole planetary system of the cosmos as there is within us; and there is no "bigger" of the Universe, with us as the "smaller." We are the whole Universe. And each one of us, each part of the Universe, reflects the glory of the other and the glory of the whole—the glory of the universal Love and Law.

So we've been given a gift, and we need to *practice* it. It's always interesting to me when someone new is brought to our teaching: this is because someone who is practicing it is telling someone else what they have done and how they've used it. So the work is a sort of counseling together, a loving together. In other words, the work, then, is the teaching and the practice.

That's what it's all about.

Your Secret Place

ONE OF THE THINGS I have always loved about the Science of Mind is that it demonstrates that we have the ability to think to make things happen . . . to set things in motion . . . to control our own destiny. And we say that because God is all, therefore we have that Mind which is of God, which gives us the right to set these things in motion. Yet we keep forgetting that, when all else fails, we can cut past the experiences, the effects, the conditions, and we can go deeply to a Place where, although it has always seemed vague, we can communicate, dialogue, and feel the comforting, directing Presence of God. And this is where it all happens.

At this moment all of us are walking a roadway—a roadway of life on earth. And we'll continue to walk it—some a little longer than others. Children a lot longer. But whether we're young or whether we're old, every one of us has had difficulties on this roadway. That is why we turn to our teaching. Not to have a magic wand or to get answers as though from fortune cookies. No, we turn to our teaching and turn our difficulty over to the Presence of God from our Secret Place, and it ceases to be a difficulty. It becomes rather an *invitation* to allow the

Presence of God to move through us. And only from a strong source of energy—from the Secret Place of the Most High—can it emerge.

I have found that what we do is *transcend* our experiences, not go up and come right back down in them. This we do by entering into that quiet Place, by whatever means. Whether we sit in a park and look at the little children, hear them laughing, see the birds; whether we look at the trees or the flowers in our meditation garden; whether we come to church and block out the sounds of traffic; or whether we just sit with a quiet cup of coffee staring at a painting or a portrait that inspires us: that's where it is. We find this Place within ourselves; and when we proceed from it, we return to our true identity, our individuality. Then we can answer why we feel good, why things begin to happen.

Now the old idea of prayer was developed in order for us to find the Secret Place. I have always felt that the old form of prayer was nothing more than a series of pleadings or supplications to a capricious, invisible being that we call God—one who might or might not grant what we wanted. There was also a certain kind of moral policing that prevented some types of prayers and encouraged others, because the prayers wouldn't be answered if we didn't clean them up properly—such things as our "sins of omission." (I have always defined sins of omission as *things we've always wanted to do but didn't dare do* because somebody would scold us.)

There's the kind of prayer associated with the little boy who looked longingly at his friend's dog. Christmas was coming, and the little boy said to his friend, "I want a dog for Christmas, but my folks say I can't have one." The friend looked at him and said, "You didn't ask right. Ask for a baby brother—then you'll get the dog."

Now there have been hundreds of people, thousands, millions who have prayed their way, even with the old form of prayer, to find that Secret Place. They kept on praying, kept on praying, until by sheer force they entered the doorway. But it's not necessary to use such tremendous force. Perseverance may be necessary, but it's not the answer. The answer lies in the feeling that *I freely and easily move in a world of people, I move in a world of experiences—and all these are God's delight in creation.*

Dr. Ernest Holmes was fond of the writings of the great scientist Alexis Carrel, who said that belief acts like physical law, because it's a law of cause and effect. He became a great man of science through his belief—he was actually at one with the teaching of Religious Science, although he didn't know it—and the technical skills he had. He began to seek divine guidance for his problems. He looked for that Secret Place, a place where his mind would be attuned and aligned with the Mind of God, where the harmony and the rhythm would release those ideas he needed. And so he proved that there is a power that anyone can use.

The Secret Place is a place all of us have been forced to go to whether we admit it or not, time after time. And it's a very comforting thing when we can say from the Secret Place, "I know there's Something that heals and blesses and restores and renews; and in this Secret Place I know there is an infinite Something that loves me and gives of Its love without withholding." Yes, there's a comfort to it, a safe harbor, *and* it's the place where everything that happens originates. Jesus said, "My peace I give unto you." We feel safe because in Truth there can be no other thing but safety. Ernest Holmes used to say to me time after time, "George, nobody ever got lost, because if God is all there is, where could I go to get lost?"

And so we seek that Secret Place. But wherever God is, there it is; and so, it's *everywhere.* God is in and through all of us. And if "it works" in one way for one person, it works in all ways for all persons.

That Secret, quiet Place: I've thought long about it. I recall that the Navy aircraft carriers have had for the last fifty years quiet rooms where briefings can take place. They're padded. They're quiet. You can sit in the quiet when they're not being used and *feel* the quiet giving you the strength, the understanding, and the realization that there's Something greater than you are—Something that shuts out the sounds of war.

There's always a "quiet room." For the Navy to have developed it and put it on their carriers of destruction and peace-keeping, the idea had to come from somewhere—only not just the mind of man, but from the Mind of God. Somebody wanted to duplicate that "quiet room" that we have within us—where the turmoil and the confusion is all dissolved into what we desire to be.

Now we in this teaching believe you can't conceive of God being more with one person than with another. It's equally distributed and equally available. Thus we need to throw away the old ideas of God—but not throw away God. And we need to throw away the old ideas of prayer—but not prayer itself. We do it by attention, by knowing, by desire, and by meditation. In one prayer, the 23rd Psalm, David, the ruler of Israel, sought a quiet Place that you can actually *feel* when you say, "The Lord is my shepherd; I shall not want. He maketh me to lie down in green pastures: he leadeth me beside the still waters. He restoreth my soul." That's the Secret, quiet Place that David sought.

And in another prayer, the 46th Psalm, are these words: "Be still, and know that I am God: I will be exalted among the heathen, I will be exalted in the earth." When we do that, we find that our prayer is a redirection of the creativity that emerged from the Secret Place; and there is a stoppage of self-ruin. This is where we finally accept the invitation to grow and change.

The Friend Within

ONE OF THE MOST serious maladies of our city and country is a disease called loneliness. We can live with somebody and still be lonely. The truth is, we are probably using it as a retreat to avoid facing the realities of our living world of experience. It's a good way to escape the disillusionment we have about our jobs, home, food, wars, taxes, government. It all gets to be too much to bear. So we retreat, and then we feel miserable.

I remember how, in my own experience years ago, I had the opportunity to move from having a family with me to being alone. For a while I was miserable because I *wasn't* miserable! Then for a while I was *just plain miserable*, suffering beautifully—until I suddenly realized: *there's more than this; I am not alone. There's something that, if I can find it again, will be with me and guide me and sustain me.*

I did a lot of praying. I had a tree that grew outside my patio that I called *Charlie*, and I used to say to myself when I went out there, "See? I'm not alone! Charlie waves his branches and bends down to kiss my hand."

(This is what happens when you get lonely.)

I began to realize that *there's something more*. Finally, I remembered that as I talk to life and talk to people, I am talking to *myself*; and there God is, talking to God.

That's what we believe in: there is something that is always there, closer than hands and feet, and *always there*—a living God with a voice that says, "You and I are bigger than all of this." We begin to seek it—and to find it.

In our loneliness there's a continuing combative urgency to struggle for security. When we struggle for security within, the survival struggles that we make in our world of living become larger and larger. We feel low, we feel lonely; we look at the papers and the media, and we see these fantastic sums of two billion dollars, eight billion dollars, forty-six billion dollars to save the banking system. They throw these figures around and tell you the world currency markets are declining. Everybody is scrambling. And all you say is, "Is this all there is?! What's the use?" You tell yourself there's nothing that guarantees any security.

At that moment you are forgetting one of the basic principles of our teaching: there is always a Presence, there is always a Friend, a Partner—even a business Partner—that guides and directs you. Then you run into somebody on the street, and you're looking down, and he says, "I'm optimistic about things," but his face drops, and you say to him, "If you're so optimistic, why do you look so worried?" And his answer is, "I'm pessimistic about my optimism!" And that only adds more frustration.

Then you "talk over" your problems. You say, "I'm going to talk to Mary; maybe she can help me." You telephone and there's no answer. You call someone else to see what happened to Mary. Well, Mary moved away; she's not there. Then you try to talk to someone at your place of work and they tell you,

"Don't bother me, I've got enough of my own problems." And then you walk along the street and you begin to feel lonelier and lonelier and lonelier.

Instead of talking over our problems with a "friend," we seek a Friend that we can talk to and really have as a *Friend*. You have this Friend: *within yourself*.

We teach that there is a spiritual Presence right within you. That if you will allow It to, It will help you enjoy living, enjoy life. We tell you that you've got an *authority* within you to do whatever you want to. What's important is whether you find it; what you do about it. I know *I've* had to look for it, find it, and—every time I forget—go back to it.

We have a Friend that says, "I am going to give you the ability, the power, and dominion to choose what you want. You can choose to retreat; you can choose to suffer. Or you can choose to love."

You can choose to reject life or you can choose to take up your bed and go out and touch life as all of us want to do.

We have a teaching that says there is a Love somewhere where we can feel an invisible "ledge" up above the pressure around us. We don't know what it is. But there is the same feeling you get when you love a dog or an animal you treat: *there is something that responds*. We have a teaching that says *that's there for you*. We have something that says *you have the ability to pray effectively*. And when you pray, you're talking to God. You are talking to that Friend, and letting that Friend come forth. And Its voice says, "Remember I have told you: you are a loving, living expression of Me."

I've got to tell you that sometimes some of my talks with God are not the kind they write up in the textbooks. I talk to Him sometimes and I say, "Why *me*? What's the reason for it? Why do I have to go through this? Haven't I always served You? What do You want from me? What did I do?" And you listen and you listen, and suddenly that voice says, "Why *not* you? Who do you think you are?'' Then you begin to realize that there *is* a Presence.

Our whole system is based upon prayer and treatment and right mental attitudes. We know that our attitudes cluster together and reflect our personality, that there's no avenging force denying us self-expression. The still voice is always saying, ''Whenever you're ready, I'm here.'' All you have to do is pick up the mental telephone and say, ''Good morning, God; I'm here.'' And so long as the good that we want doesn't contradict the general welfare of the Universe, that good is given.

You see, our work is a combination of intellect, of techniques, of formulas, of proven principles, and of feeling. All of our work is directed to the end that we reveal the divine intuition and courage within us. Because, when we allow these to govern our lives, we can say, ''My Friend God is walking down the street to me. My Friend God is going to work with me. My Friend God is with me.'' There's a deep sense of awareness of our nature. We arrive at the perfect assurance, the perfect faith; and as we have it, we stop contemplating how lonely we are.

This is good, for we tend to give power to that which is true as a fact of experience; but mere *experience* is not the same as *truth*. And sometimes we get so busy with our ''facts'' and our intellect that we throw out the eternal Facts and start rearranging everything. Wife to her husband at a social gathering: ''I wish you'd stop correcting me, Roscoe. Half the fun of remembering the good old days is rearranging them!''

There's much to be said for claiming ''I am my own best friend.'' We're not talking egotistically. With the scriptural ''I Am,'' you're invoking the idea that the Christ in you is your Friend forever more. And within me—within all of us—is something that says, ''You're right!'' Then why don't we find it?

I think, then, we may be ready, all of us, to make the decision to give our unqualified consent to the healing power of the Friend within; to give our consent to live affirmatively; to walk out and say good morning to people we see in the street; to say, "Thank you, God, for this day." You go to work and say, "My Friend is with me." You see people walking down the street smiling, self-confident. If you look, you can almost see they're smiling because they've got a Friend with them—that Friend that we all have.

So we turn from the so-called solace of rejecting the world like the ancient monks and hermits who used to go up on top of a hill, dig a hole, and stay there because they couldn't face the reality of living. That's the equivalent of what we do when we are lonely. We create our cave and crawl into it.

Instead, we open some part of our mind. We say to ourselves, "Didn't all these great people teach us that fear, sickness, limitation, and death are inventions of our minds?" Our Friend God didn't give them to us. Maybe we have been thinking in terms of effects, experiences, and not in terms of causation, Truth, and how joyous life can be. And so we have taken what is the very essence of our teaching and its power, and we've said, "I choose the power to be lonely. I am going to go to my room and nobody is going to get me out of there. The world is no good!"

As a young man, I went to Gettysburg Academy in Gettysburg, Pa. In the room next to mine was a friend, a vital young man and member of the Rifle Team by the name of John Paul Murphy. One night I heard a loud shot. The captain of the Rifle Team had picked up a rifle that he mistakenly thought was unloaded and mock-fired it, killing the young man. That tragic act contributed in its paradoxical way to the formation of one of the great men of our times—Thomas Merton, author of *The Seven-Storey Mountain* and many other spiritual works. He was the captain. As a result, he turned to religion and entered the monastic life.

I remember something he wrote in one of his books: "I wonder if there are twenty men in the world who see things as they really are." And then he added, "I don't believe there are twenty such people in the world; but there *must* be one, there *must* be two. *They* are the ones who will hold everything together and keep the Universe from falling apart.''

When we do our treatment work, it takes only one of us to *know*. I could stand here before you, attempt to set the mold in healing prayer, and ask you to unite with me in what I'm speaking about—but it's not me doing it. It's the Friend within. *One* person has such total, absolute conviction and belief that the Friend within is there, that the healing takes place. God didn't go anywhere. God wasn't lost. We lost ourselves. We have to return to the realization of the Friend within—the Presence of an Infinite Loving God.

You know, in the process of this realization, the ones who come out of the cave of loneliness look at themselves in the mirror and say, ''What am I becoming?'' We forget that all the greats of our teaching have said we're talented; we're light, appealing people. The only reason we seem not to be is that we don't accept it. God has blessed all of us with all of the same qualities.

The Friend is available from the time of our birth through the time of our departure. We live to graduate. I've always felt that the Friend is there to guide us into our new experience. But we forget what we are.

Much of the anxiety is in our physical world, and this is causing us to retreat—because of the collective thought of seemingly impossible problems. But if we all got up and said, ''I am my own best Friend,'' then we could look at the brother alongside of us and say, ''He's my Friend too.'' You see, we study, we work, we *use*—until we believe that there *is* a Friend there who *will* answer what we think about, including what we think of ourselves: are we spiritual beings, with the right to love and sing and dance? Are we *happy*?

Picture yourself on an airliner. It's smoggy as you approach the airport. Now, do you want a pilot who is ''broadminded,'' free to do what he wants, to fly as he chooses with no regard for the instruments or the radar beam; or do you want him to stay on the beam with strictness and focus of attention? Don't you want that focus while he is piloting the airplane? We must focus on our understanding and say, "I shut all other things out; for there is a Friend within."

Most of the work in the church, in the classroom, begins at the house or the apartment. I can't tell my neighbor, "Your back yard is dirty; will you please clean it up?" He only looks over the fence and says, "Look at *your* yard!" No—make friends with yourself before worrying about the others.

My next question is, do we really like our self? Do we look in the mirror and say, "Hey, you did a great job today! I'm going to keep you!" Or do we say, "Whoops! You really fouled it up!" We react when somebody or something threatens. But we can't be threatened when our Friend is there in our life. There can be no greater unity than "I and my Father are One"—the unity between you and this inner Friend.

The table has been spread for us "in the wilderness of human thought." But the table was always there, spread wide. The Psalmist said, "My cup runneth over," and the cup of joy placed on God's table runneth over indeed. Your Friend "laughs at disaster, triumphs over human failure, and mocks the grave." The Friend within you lives in a state of *cause*.

I want to share with you some words from one of Dr. Ernest Holmes' favorite little books, taught in our classes—*Your Invisible Power*:

> The Friend within you lives in a state of poise, He is above fear, He is beyond hurt, He is sufficient unto Himself.
>
> The Friend within you is continuously looking after your well-being. He always wishes you to be happy, to be well, to be radiant. Being the very fountain of your life, this Friend is a luminous Presence, forevermore

emerging from pure Spirit, evermore expanding your consciousness. He is the High Counselor, the Eternal Guide. He is your intellect, the essence of its understanding, the nicety of its calculation, the appreciation of its temperament.

There can be no greater unity than exists between you and this inner Friend. . . . Trust Him, then, today, and you may trust Him for all the tomorrows yet to come. . . .

Your personality is an out-picturing of the impressions which you have received from this inner Friend, this Deep Personality. . . . You are an incarnation of this Person, this Presence, and this Power. . . .

He is an unconquerable hero. He who keeps silent watch within you lifts your consciousness to the realization that you are forever protected, forever safe, forever perfect.

Belief That Does More than Believe

ONE OF THE THREE basic desires of all of us as humans is to be able to pray and establish a communion with Something greater than we are—for we all have a basic belief in the Presence of God, even if we would rather be in Dodger Stadium than in church. We all basically believe in, and desire the establishment of, a communion in prayer with this Presence—because over tens of thousands of years the race has had a primordial instinct that tells us there is Something more. We find that people turn to our teaching not really just to get a job or to get a husband or a wife or a boyfriend or a girlfriend but to be able to establish in prayer that which can give them the comfort and the harmony and the peace they need in a society that is moving tremendously fast.

The basic principle for the practice of this teaching is that we are living in a spiritual Universe now—that we're governed by laws of Intelligence, and that that Intelligence, acting in law mathematically, will respond with mechanical regularity to the spontaneity of our thinking. And perhaps it's more emphatic in this teaching than in any other that this is the basis of all demonstration.

I think that basically we all believe, even though we doubt, even though we say we're agnostic. We believe that there is Something creative that acts upon our spoken word or our thought. Call it a divine Principle. Call it a universal Subjectivity, Subconscious. Call it the Soul of the Universe. Call it the Law of Life—or just don't call it anything. But it's there. And if it acts upon our thought the way we speak our thought—and therefore through the even more effective method of communion in terms of *prayer* by thought or affirmation—then we can use all the principles and laws of the Universe.

We need this communion in times like these—and what I'm saying is what was said thousands of years before Jesus. They have found stone inscriptions complaining about all the same old things: children no longer respect their parents, the world has lost all of its moral values, etc. Every ten years, of course, that's repeated. But our *reaction* is most important. We are forced to pray because of our *reaction*; and we tend to react only when we're threatened. Our reaction to experiences and circumstances determines how we measure our weakness and strength. Even the direction of our prayer is determined by how we react to our experience.

Some of the old-fashioned understanding of prayer always shocks me when I have people who have studied in our teaching for months and years come into my office and say, "My prayers aren't working." I ask them to give me a run-down of their last prayer, what they said. And invariably it reveals an act of supplication, of begging—an act of undirected thinking and emotion—a prayer addressed to a separate, far-off Being that is thought to be capable of giving or withholding in a capricious way. And no special effort to maintain a correct belief and prevent the destructive from materializing.

But our approach is really very simple. We recognize the omniscience, omnipresence, and omnipotence of God—and that we are an expression of God. We also have a definite idea of what we desire. We've learned that by coupling these desires with constructive affirmative statements, we can bring about their realization. We have a belief and we maintain it, trying as best as we can to eliminate all the destructive, unhappy thoughts. So prayer is the time, the process, and the method necessary to the changing of our thoughts—a clearing of all doubts, destructiveness, and fear, recognizing the ever-presence of a living, loving Force, a living, loving God. A pianist has to understand the science of music; a pilot has to understand the science of flight; a mathematician, the science of numerical relationships. And so there is a science of prayer; not a cold technology, but a feeling of warmth in the realization of, and the total surrender to, that invisible Something. These are activated whenever we spend our time recognizing them.

I have found that most people think they are not good enough. But we're all good enough to be able to pray, to even surpass the statistic that Elaine St. Johns and William Parker wrote about in their book *Prayer Can Change Your Life*—a 72-percent effectiveness. And we're certainly spiritual enough. I don't know how much more spiritual we can be than simply to believe that God is all, that love is natural—to love ourselves and one another, and to love and adore a Presence greater than we are, knowing that God lives in us and we live in God. And I really don't think we have to worry about any of that, because God, as we believe, is all there is. You and I didn't make it that way, but we *can* accept it. It's a simplicity.

I can hear someone saying, "What do I have to do now? Take another class so I can get more spiritual? It seems to me I've been taking classes for months, and it hasn't made any difference." Let me tell you, I know people who have studied for 15 years and they still don't know anything. They haven't got it in the *feeling* and in the *conviction*. They're standing on streetcorners making vain repetitions. Ernest Holmes always said that the purpose of classes was to expand the mind in mental stretching exercises so we become more aware of its vastness. But there really isn't enough in all the classes, even though we teach them for years, to make a decent bowl of clam chowder—because it's got to be within *you*.

We all know "enough." If you know how to think, you know enough. If you know how to believe that there is Something greater than you are, in total simplicity, then you know enough. If you know enough to articulate, to visualize, or to paint a picture of a desire, you know enough. The whole question, though, comes down to this: do you *do* it? And do you believe, when you pray, that your word is acted upon by a Law of mind and that the thought behind it is a seed planted in a bed of pure creative causation that will bear fruit?

But perhaps your next thought is "I agree with all that, but how do I do it? Do I concentrate on it?" No, it is not concentration. Concentration means to bring to a center. Anybody can bring anything to a center if they want to. And I'm not criticizing the idea of concentration. I dropped it years ago when I decided to remove myself from the intellectual temptation of manipulation. You may say, "But doesn't a mathematician concentrate the law of mathematics?" No. He or she *uses* it.

Forget concentration. When you take a seed and plant it, you don't concentrate on the idea of the whole creative essence. You don't concentrate; the dirt is getting on it! The nitrates in the soil are acting on it! You don't concentrate on that. You take the seed and you plant it—because you believe it's going to grow. You don't "hold" the thought; that's an impossibility. You *release* thinking—to be acted upon in a great, creative Universe. You can't *will* anything to happen. If you and I and all of us put together decided that we would *will* something to take place, we'd all drop dead from exhaustion. If we decided that we were going to *will* the round earth into a flat surface (like before Columbus), the only thing that would get flat would be the top of our heads.

What you do is affirm and believe in the affirmation and the words you are speaking. If you truly believe that as you speak an idea or word it will happen, it happens. I don't know what the process is. I don't know what makes eating a ham sandwich become tissues and hair and teeth and bones. And I certainly don't attempt to *concentrate* on it. But I know that it happens.

What we are considering here is probably most difficult because we have to *believe*—not in a forlorn hope, nor in a mystical something, but in the immutable principle of a Law that reacts with regularity to the spontaneity of your thought. And here is where our teaching and training enter in. The other day there were some things I wasn't particularly happy about, and I said, "Nothing happens the way I want it to." I was disappointed and angry. Finally I said to myself, "Look, little guy" (because we're all but a pinprick dot in the infinite scheme of things), "why are you getting so hot? Why are you getting so disappointed?" And I finally said, "This is ridiculous; something good is going to come of it all. I'll just forget about it for now." So the belief that we're talking about is *acceptance* within the assurance of a principle, call it a law, that is proven to exist and that works all the time.

Frequently in class I ask people to give a meditation or affirmation and they tell me they're not prepared, that they'll work on it during the week and write one out. You don't have to *prepare* it; whatever your feeling is can be translated into words. But you do have to *believe* it when you're giving this kind of prayer. We have learned in this teaching that you never really pray for anybody else. That's an impossibility—because if you're standing *here*, and the water is *there*, you're not going to get wet. If you're standing here and trying to make the water move to you, it's no good. To get wet, you've got to walk down and get into the water. But notice: if you pour purple dye in the water *here*, that purple dye will spread to every part of the water.

It's the same in our prayer work. We have to pray to *ourself* before we can establish anything with anybody else. Once we've done that, we can rest assured that if there's one Action, if there's one Energy, then what we believe in Truth affects what another believes. If it's in some situation that needs harmonizing—and I don't know anybody living who doesn't have a problem with harmonizing—we have to say, "This that I'm thinking, this that I'm *believing*, now moves through my home, my work, my relationships. There is a unity of love, there is a harmony, there is a cooperation; and this word removes every sense of confusion, doubt, uncertainty, antagonism, resistance, resentment—whatever has to be surendered." You've got to put it into the form of your own words. And believe it.

It sounds funny to say, but what you are seeking to demonstrate is already there, like water in an ice cube. If I take an ice cube and hold it in my hand, the ice cube is going to melt. My hand won't have an ice cube, it will have liquid. Similarly, whatever it is you're trying to correct, you can't put harmony into the essence of it; *it's already there.* If you think of it as melting like the ice cube, then it reverts to the liquid of pure Spirit— because all forms of experience are but an ice cube in the warm, flowing energy of time.

There is no opposite to God. There's only one Power, one Force—and as you and I use it constructively, it operates for us. *You* are the person, *here and now* is the place. *Today* is the time, *this* is the moment, and the word is in *your mind.* It's an affirmative word that you speak—but you've got to believe it and identify with it, want it to happen and then let it go. Don't wait until you "know more." Don't wait until you finish more years of study. Don't wait until you "get more spiritual." You're as spiritual now as you ever will be. Don't wait until you "get more understanding."

It's there; don't wait. *Don't wait!* The stream of causation is *here, now,* and *forevermore.* If you don't plant the seeds in the garden soil, you won't get anything. You've got the soil ready. *Plant* the seeds, and *know* that they flourish. Think about what it is that you want to have happen. You're probably in the mood *right now.* You've got the soil clear of weeds, and you're not conscious of anything else. Think of it, visualize it. Don't be afraid to experiment; don't be afraid to dare.

When you get finished praying for yourself, pray for someone else. It can't hurt; and you can't tell: someone may walk up to you in the next couple of days and say, ''Boy! You know that thing I had? All of a sudden I feel great!'' It can't hurt. And you don't have to take credit for it. After all, *you* didn't do it; you recognized a spiritual law that always existed, and you put yourself in alignment with it. The law of electricity might have been used by Moses had he only understood it.

Emerson said: ''Is not prayer a study of Truth, a sally of the soul into the unfound infinite?'' Prayer is constructive because it enables us to establish closer contact with the Fountain of Wisdom. We are less likely to be influenced by appearances around us. Prayer is essential, not necessarily to the ''salvation'' of the soul (for the soul is never lost), but to the conscious well-being of the soul that doesn't understand itself. There is vitality in our communion with the Infinite which is productive of the highest good, just as fire warms the body, as food strengthens it, and as sunshine raises our spirits. There is a subtle transfusion of some invisible force in such communion, weaving itself into the very warmth of our mentalities. This conscious comingling of our thought with Spirit is essential to the well-being of us. We all need this conscious union with the Infinite.

Cause and effect are but two sides of thought; and Spirit, being all, is both Cause and Effect. Prayer, then, is its own answer. The Bible tells us that ''Before they call, I will answer.'' Before our prayer is framed in words, God has already answered it. But if our prayer is one of *partial* belief, then there is only a *tendency* towards its goal. And if next we *wholly* doubt, then there is *no* answer at all. In dealing with mind, we're dealing with a force we cannot fool. What to do? Learn to go deeply within yourself and speak as though there were a Presence there that knows. Take the necessary time to penetrate this inner chamber of consciousness and to unearth this hidden Cause, this Spirit that is always flowing through us.

Decide and Do

One of the salient points of our teaching is that the power of choice is governed by no one other than ourselves. Part of the creative process that Ernest Holmes taught so fervently is that if we don't like where we are or what the situation is, we can make a decision and select something else.

We know that at the level of awareness we can analyze a situation, dissect it, and then select the movement we wish to make. We know that when we select it *and believe it* and turn it over to God, the creative process of that choice will bring it into form. We also know that when we say Yes to something, we're saying No to something else. In a word, we know that our entire life is based on *movement*.

Ernest Holmes used to say that we *fall* forward in evolution. So we move forward, we move upward with every choice we make. If it's incorrect, we can turn around and select another method of movement. So decision is important to all of us in this teaching; and one of the first things we have to do, then, is to work at this level mentally—to tell ourselves what we want from the future, what we want from God. And if we don't know, we won't go anywhere and we won't attain anything.

We make a decision or we do *not* make a decision. If the old past is not exactly a comfortable shoe, we at least know where it pinches—and we don't know what will happen with the new shoe (decision). But it is not hard for us to recognize how silly this is, because when we suppress that divine urge of decision and growth, we certainly show it.

You may have a decision to make to accept yourself for what you are. You may have a decision to make because you feel gloomy and depressed. You may have a decision to make to experience the joy of new living and new experience. You may want your health, and again you have a decision to make—to irrevocably accept the fact that your body is a temple of the Living God.

You may have a decision to make, wanting your marriage to work though your spouse doesn't like you or treat you right. You may have a decision to make to know that you want to give yourself to the highest and fullest degree possible—and that in giving, you are giving not to get something, but because you know it is right for you to give. Or you may have a decision to make about a habit you have that you want to get rid of, and your decision is to separate the idea of what is harmful from what isn't.

What do you want from the future? Because when you make a decision to *not* make a decision, you are holding up the growth and expression of God within you. You may have a decision to make to reaffirm that God sustains, maintains, and directs you. Can you accept that God has given no spirit of fear—only that of power, of love, and of a sound mind—? Because if you don't you won't go anywhere: the decision will have been made to do nothing.

And how can you get anything if you don't know what it is you want to get? So you've got to decide *to know what it is that you want*. And if we have a clear conviction, we need to apply it to ourselves in the sight of God; and happy are we if we can make our decision with clear conscience and consciousness.

So the nature of God, the nature of man and of being is perfect and harmonious and whole. And this is our work: to make a decision to let that nature reveal itself. We are all of us surrounded by tremendous opportunities to decide. But even though we're surrounded by them, there are also seemingly limitless temptations and traps. So we must *decide* that we live in a world so rich with possibility that unless we exercise at least some degree of diligence—having an understanding of our decision-making power—we may find ourselves only back in the same old position.

Yes, we *do* have to make a commitment, we *do* have to decide what it is we want to be committed to. Heraclitus claimed that the bitterest sorrow we can know is to aspire to much and achieve nothing. I agree in part, but I might rephrase it by saying that the bitterest sorrow is to aspire to do much and to do it, and then to discover it wasn't worth doing to begin with. So again the decision, the yes or the no. It's not only what we do but also what we *don't* do for which we are held accountable by the very power of the creative thought. If you choose unwisely or allow others to thrust decisions upon you, it's still the same thing.

So we need to do two things. We need to think *where we are;* and then we need to *evaluate*. These are requisite for any decision we need to make. I'm reminded of the minister who was talking with one of his congregation, a hard-working cleaning woman. He told her how glad he was to see her in her place in church on Sunday, so attentive to the sermon. "Yes," she replied, "it's so restful, after a hard week, to come to church, sit down on a soft cushion, and not have to think about anything."

I've had that experience.

No, we need to think—after first listening to the still, small voice of inner wisdom. There are many half-truths along the way in making any decision—while we may secretly be looking for an excuse to not decide. And the excuse(s) may sound convincing to us until we see that the same old thing is repeating itself. The opposite of this, of course, is jumping to conclusions instead of true decision-making.

Have you heard the story of the fisherman whose wedding ring slipped off into the water as he struggled to get a big fish into his boat? Some three or four days later he was fishing in the same spot and he hooked a good-size fish. Anticipating the pleasure of having it for supper, he took it home immediately. As he was cleaning it, his knife cut into something hard and solid.

It was his finger.

Did you jump to a conclusion there?

We have a Friend within us who lives in a state of poise, above the fear of not making a decision—or of jumping to conclusions—and this Friend is always there to be called upon and to help us.* Help us, too, in the matter of the fears that arise because of the push to decide that we want something more.

Probably the first emotion any of us experiences is fear. There's fear, I'm told, incident to the process of childbirth. All of a sudden the infant is snatched into the open where the beginning of the growth experience must take place. And so the baby is picked up and patted, loved, reassured—and begins a process of decision-making. But fear can dog baby's little steps—and ours—in two principal ways that prevent making a decision.

The first is what we see around us, threatening, attacking. By its very nature, it is *rational* enough for us to have this fear. It serves a useful function, revealing to us real dangers. Still, we can't afford to say, "I'm just going to sit here and not make a decision. That way I'll be protected and won't have to face real dangers." No, we can't "just sit there."

The second way fear prevents us from making decisions is

* See "The Friend Within," p. 22.

through *irrational* fear. This is the kind of fear that inhibits and cripples us, forgetting that "in God we trust." This isn't a fear of real danger; it's a fear of *ourselves*. And a fear that we *project*. This often takes the form of seeing ourselves *without*—without money, jobs, other people—the fear that we "don't have it" to succeed in a very active world, with the added fear of international developments and Lord knows how many other things— our children; other children.

Someone asked me, "How do you make *your* decisions?" I said, that about 80 percent of the time I'll try to reason them out. The other 20 percent—where I haven't gotten a rational answer —I'll flip a coin and go whichever way the coin says. However I'm quick to add that when I let a toss of the coin guide me, it is *not* the decision I should have made.

For some people, coin-tossing works. Professor Rhine, the famous parapsychologist of Duke University, years ago conducted experiments from which he concluded that people by their own thinking unknowingly control the toss of the coin or the throw of the dice. While I've never been quite able to accept that, it must afford at least some encouragement for those who favor tossing a coin.

The truth is that every decision you've got to make must be made from the emotional need to give you a sense of comfort or security; so every decision must have the fulfillment of that requirement within it. Even the decision how to vote, which so many believe is based upon merely cold logic, is grounded on a need for security, identification, the hero ideal, and the need of a loving Father that cares. For there's Something within that tells us, "Be not afraid, for I am always with you." Yes, Something within wants to convince us of this to the highest degree possible.

There's Something within that's an echo of the Universe, of the song of God. There's something within that's an echo of the planets in the solar system. There's Something within that's an echo of the wind, the song of the birds, the sound of the crickets, the warmth of the sun.

But there's something within that says, "I am not just a compartmentalized little individual." There's a mental echo that says, "Everything in the Universe, everything in all the worlds, is in here." There's Something within that says, "I am the first moment of your creation—a divine and spiritual Self that has everything within It. I haven't planted it in an organ, I haven't planted it in an artery or a vein, I haven't planted it in a bone; but I *have* planted it in the essence of My Life, which is expressing through you. I seek an area of expression, and as you allow this to happen, you express Me to the highest and fullest degree."

Decide and allow yourself to be the self you want to be. When you are not yourself, you've adopted all those little gimmicks of humankind—guilt, fear, anxiety, and insecurity. And so maybe you say to the Voice, "I've done wrong—I've suppressed myself. I haven't allowed You to come forth, my part in this is terrible!" But the Voice says, "Be not afraid; for I am always with you."

So it's perhaps the most important action of your mind, the most important action of the creative thought process, to make the conscious decision to move on to the next experience. We move from experience to experience. We live in a world of mess and clean up. When we sit too long on a decision without making it, we get a mess and then we clean it up and we "progress" through life this way. And so each time you make a decision, remember that you're prepared for a bigger thing to handle for a still bigger decision.

Like all of us, I've looked back through my life and found some parts I've liked, some parts I haven't liked. And like all of us, I've wondered what would have happened if I'd made different decisions at critical junctures of my pathway. The answer that has come to me, of course, is that I am where I am today because of the string of decisions I have made. Without them, I wouldn't be where I am, and I wouldn't be me. So the question boils down to: could any single decision have been different? "No," says my Voice; "the decision you made at that time was for your growth at that time. And a deep need determined your decision."

All of us could spend a lot of time wringing our hands and bemoaning a lot of our decisions, but that would only be foolish. That merely re-creates the agony. We need to make a decision at *this* moment. If I continue to find fault with my past, I'm continuing to find fault with my own soul.

We come to the Science of Mind teaching because we have lessons to learn. The divine echo within impells us along certain pathways—paths that will give us a chance to move in trust from one decision to another. We can look at this from so many different directions and in a lot of ways. If nondecision is due to anxiety and fear, it will prove contagious and produce all kinds of unhappy results. But if we take the opposite tack, why shouldn't affirmative, constructive mental attitudes produce the opposite result?

What we're *really* struggling with, then, is a sense of lack. We pay lip service—"I believe in God," "I trust God," "I trust the Power of God"—but we really *don't*; we are still governed by the material world around us. And therefore what we *really* need is a deep conviction that there *is* a Power greater than we are, and that we can use It for our good. *There has to come a conviction that God is where I am and where all of us are.* And God will always be there, whether we fade into the dust of antiquity or not.

Base our decisions on ourselves and the truth of God, and we live. Base our decisions on others' opinions and we die. Let's make our decision based also on the destination, not on the route to it. Because once the decision has been made, the route will reveal itself. Elijah, in First Kings, has these lines: "How long halt ye between two opinions? If the Lord be God, follow him: but if Baal, then follow him.''

Let's unite in that which is so common to all of us in this teaching—an ability to enter deeply within ourselves, to recognize that there is One Creative Power, that each one of us has the use of It, and that each one of us is a part of the other, while nonetheless an individual. For we are unique individualizations of the same Thing. And in this knowledge, then, we make a decision to respond to the echo, the sound, the harmony—to accept the real Life of God; to dedicate ourselves to the freedom from inaction; to know that within us there's one Power, One Presence—healing, renewing, guiding, directing, and sustaining us. Knowing this, we can accept it and commit ourselves to it from this moment.

Once More with Feeling: Love

LOVE HOLDS US TOGETHER. We know that only when we get the debris out of the way and allow the pure, unadulterated, living, loving God to express through us, everything is good. The rest is just a theory. We're so very glib when we say God is Love. But the only way we know whether God is Love is when our arms are around each other. I've learned that when I feel blue, I could put my arms around a child and then, in that sweet innocence, they hug me back. *I can feel God hugging me back.* That's the only way we know about it.

But usually we just fling out statements like "God is Love." It reminds me of the young man who said to his lady intended, "I love you; you're beautiful. Will you fly away with me and marry me?"

She looked at him and said, "Will you give up everything for me?"

He said, "Oh yes!"

"Will you always be at my side?"

"Oh yeah!"

Then she said, "Will you throw yourself from the highest mountain into the raging sea for me?"

He said, "No."

She looked at him and said, "I thought you said you loved me, that you'd give up everything for me."

He said, "Yes; but my love is an *undying* love."

John Powell of Loyola Marymount, a Jesuit priest, has said that love is sharing, caring, supporting, and allowing for growth. God shares, cares, supports, and allows us to grow, with a permissive Self-willingness that yields all there is to us. When we yield angers, fears, and resentments, then the Universe yields more to us. The rest is mere theory.

I read a book years ago on the Ways and Powers of Love. After twenty years the author had 360 and said that there were more. But it is still one and the same thing. And sometimes I think it's something we don't know anything about. We're so prone in our practice and teaching to study *techniques*, to study *methods*, and to forget there's *feeling*. We can pray, we can treat, we can repeat affirmations until we are blue in the face; but without love there's nothing. And so it is we find that when we're not living the life we feel we would like to live and are riddled with fears, we age and curl up, have insomnia, and finally have to go to church—in order to catch up on our sleep. But when we express love, we find that our face, our skin, our hair, our eyes take on a vitality, a glow; and so we live more and we love more.

Whenever I think about fears, I think about the great airliner that flew into a violent thunderstorm and was bumping along. One nervous lady in the plane happened to be sitting next to a clergyman (she could tell; he had one of those collars that went around the other way) and turned to him for comfort. She said, "Can't you do something? you're a clergyman." He looked at her through a soft smile and said, "Madam, I'm in *sales*, not in *management*."

You know, we stress hugs a lot. Ours must be some of the *huggingest* churches in America. Everybody hugs everybody else. Strangers feel it. It came from a Scandinavian word—*hugga*.

It's used on special occasions to signify joy when people come together for good. And the English language, one of the most difficult languages because it is borrowed from so many others, got the word *hug*.

We come together and enjoy. Ours should be a joyful church. This is what we believe. This is what it's all about. I think one of the most profound things that have taken place in the last hundred years, is learning that *the capacity to love has to grow*. You know: you do it once, it's easy; you do it again, you love a little more. And again, a little more. It grows. We move away from what we think is our vulnerability and find out that there wasn't anything to be vulnerable about. We loved and we were loved back.

We all have the ability to pray and treat; we all have the ability to love. It's always there. Some people even love to *resent*. We all have that *ability*. But as we use it constructively, it's like learning how to bowl or play tennis. As we do it more often, it becomes a reflex; and the more we do it, use it—sharing, caring, supporting, and allowing for growth—we find we've lived more, longer, and greater.

There isn't anyone who cannot recognize that one of the most revealing conditions of the times seems to be an increase in violence in almost every walk of life. Violence is the positive mark of hostility. And hostility is the inevitable behavior pattern of those who feel separated from other people, from life, from God—because we know that when we are insecure and threatened, when we don't feel loved, we attack. We know that when we feel loved, we respond in kind. When we love, it comes back to us. But then the question comes, What is this thing you are talking about? What is this? People will say that it doesn't particularly mean anything to them.

I can share with you an experience I had years ago in New York. I had a little church on top of the roof of the Hotel Shelburne. One day, driving through the narrow streets with brakes

I'd forgotten to pray about in the morning, I went through the intersection and a huge truck had to brake and turn violently to avoid hitting me. The driver got out—and I thought *I* was tall and in relatively good condition; but I looked up, and here was the biggest man I had ever seen. Big this way and big that way with hands that looked like sledge-hammer mallets, scowling and swearing as he got out of the truck.

I turned and I said, "God, You'd better take care of this." This man came up to me, and you never heard what I heard for the next five minutes. (We're nice family people; I don't want to repeat it.) The essence of it was that I was stupid, I was ignorant, and I shouldn't have a drivers license. You can imagine the rest. Finally he paused for a breath, and all I could think of that came out of me was "I love you too." He looked at me, mumbled in disgust, turned, and went back to the truck and drove off.

So I learned that there *is* a power of love. But I've learned that it reveals things by the heart. We talk about "heart." The word *courage* comes from the French word *coeur*, or "heart." Heart symbolizes to us love. And so God reveals things by the heart—and by our common sense and intellect. And then we try to add them together and see if they make sense. I suppose I could talk endlessly about love, and about sharing, caring, supporting, and allowing for growth. And yet the truth of anything is not taught. It must be caught and felt. We *feel* it. Whether words have any impact or not, the feeling is what we respond to.

Love: the willing, permissive sharing of all there is. We say, "Abundance is thine: come and take it." By the principles of our teaching, we have the right to accept what is given to us; and its givingness never stops. It is unconditional givingness because its whole reason for being is love. God loves humanity—otherwise it would not have been created. It was created in that love, and therefore each one of us is a part of that, is God's love in expression.

Our receiving it sometimes is not equal to the giving. We may reject, resist, squirm, and even turn love into hate. How many people have replied to someone who said, "I want you to have this gift": "Oh no! I couldn't accept that! You shouldn't have done it! That's too much!"—and didn't take it. The would-be giver merely smiles and says, "Well, if you feel that way. . . ." But what we've done is cut off their givingness of love. We have rejected it because we didn't feel we were worthy to receive it. How many times have we hated or resented! I've done it in my life until I thought and said all that is a misdirection of love. But I felt lots better when I loved rather than hated.

I asked myself a question one time: all the great philosophers, teachers, ministers have talked about God being Love; but how do *I* know? How do *I* know? Just because somebody said so? Because John in the Bible said "God is Love"? How do *I* know God is Love? The only way I know is: *I am of God*. I am an expression of *everything*, willingly, permissively surrendered to me—and I *know* God is love to the extent of the love that I can give; and I find that when I think I have given all I can, there is still more to give.

All this instead of (as I have done at times) denying the whole thing and saying, "That's baloney!" or "*That* S.O.B.!" followed by compromising my understanding and saying, "Well, I can forgive them because they're *slightly weird*!" And that isn't true. All I am then doing is denying that God is Love, in order to affirm what I *thought* was so.

What is it I need to do, to have, to get, or to be in order to feel this love? A lot of people feel that if they focus on a discipline and a duty, that will make it happen. Because we know we have to work at it. We know it's necessary. One very frustrated man said he'd been brought up to believe he should love other people, that he should do his duty according to the good Christian doctrine, that he should practice the Ten Commandments, that he should always be respectful to others and accommodate himself to his parents and to his elders. If he did, he'd have a good, safe, comfortable life.

I wonder: comfortable in what sense of the word? It reminds me of the little girl who returned home from a friend's birthday party and reported to her parents, after they had asked how the party was, "Oh, it was a *good* party! Nobody threw up!"

Unlike my frustrated man, someone else will turn away from the "should" of convention, thinking that if he marches to an entirely different drummer, people will love him and that he will find his way to fulfillment. But he is only disconcerted, disconnected, and fails to find the love he seeks.

You see, the mystery is that you can't seek it; it is not a rare seashell, a valuable earring on the ground. It's not an *object* that you *find*—because you can't "find" it unless you *have* it. You probably know Russell Conwell's famous little booklet *Acres of Diamonds*—about the man who had been in the gold fields of Alaska and had finally made his way to the diamond fields of Africa. There he dug up quite a big stone, put it on top of his fireplace, and resumed looking for his fortune. He didn't find it and left to seek it somewhere else. When at last he made his transition, he was absolutely poverty-stricken.

His family came to claim his little cabin and sell it to pay off his debts. One of the relatives, however, was smart enough to look at the rock and have it examined. That rock turned out to be the largest diamond ever mined.

Sitting there all the while is a still greater diamond within us; and though we search and scrabble for love, there's no scarcity of it. There's *plenty* of it, wherever we might be.

We'll probably not learn to love by saying, "I am going to love!" *We have to become ready to be loved,* and to establish that readiness without fear but rather with great self-respect. I believe in a good many things, and one of them is that you and I are magnificent, loving expressions of God. I admit that I sometimes get so involved in the phenomena and effects of people, places, and things that I lay my belief aside. But I will also say that when I return to the idea of putting my arms around everyone, I feel better and I live better.

Ernest Holmes taught me that years ago. He said, "George, never go into a building, never give a talk to people, unless mentally and emotionally you put your arms around and hug them before you go onto the speaker's platform. Don't worry about them loving you. You do that and you love them, and it comes back to you a thousand times over."

The first thing we have to do in expanding our love is to look in the mirror and say, "I am a living, loving, expression of God, and I love myself because of what I am and not because of what I'm not," and then to say, "I'm a living, loving, expression of God, and I love other people for what they are and not because of what they're not." As we do this, we reflect not a saccharine, "sweet" love, but something positive and dynamic—the "glue" of the Universe that brings things *together* in our experience, according to its depth and vibration, and assembles them so that the table is full.

Love not only gives order to life. Love *is* order, love *is* harmony. Love binds together, brings together. And when that love is withdrawn, things that belong together fall between the sands of time. But time is now *for* us! See more; do more; accomplish more; love more; and *know* that that which is the perfect love of God now manifests in us. *Know* that there is a Presence. *Know* that right now where we're sitting in our minds we're hugging and embracing and loving every other individual in our world. Know it and feel it. And know that this feeling obliterates everything unlike itself, surrendering it to the Infinite to be recycled in its proper form.

Uncovering Perfection

IN TALKING WITH MANY people over the years, and in being with a lot of groups, I've become well acquainted with the effect of the inner states of mind and emotion upon the body. Years ago, I used to say that 70 percent of the illnesses of the body are caused by our own thinking. But more recently, I feel that I could say it's 99 percent and that I would be more accurate. And, too, there are those who so deeply accept their body as the vehicle for the subconscious expression of God that, no matter what they are thinking, it can be said that they have implanted a subconscious idea that manifests itself in bodily health.

Many people become interested in our teaching because they wish to heal themselves of one thing or another. Now the authority to heal is the freedom that we have to correct the abuse of this authority. We have the authority to choose whatever we wish: "choose ye therefore blessing or cursing." That is the fundamental factor of creativity and of our lives. So when we feel something with authority, whatever it may be, it will manifest itself in our body.

"Our" body is the body of God; it's not really ours. It's a marvelous instrument created by a divine power and then made subject to limited use by our intelligence and our choices. God seems to say, "I will build a house, but you will have to take care of it." And so I've always felt that the majority of our diseases are fathered in mind. The body cannot get sick; the mind gets sick, and the body reflects that. The body is a sounding board for our thoughts and feelings. When you're feeling good, your body has tone to it—a sense of vibration, harmony, and happiness—the "glow of health." When you're feeling depressed or down, the body will reflect that too. And so as the sounding board, it picks up the vibration of our thinking, which we can diminish or expand in all parts of the body.

I often think that we overlook the idea of vibration. When we enter into healing prayer, we enter into the awareness that we are created by a living, loving God. We separate ourselves from the discordant conditions and we endeavor to feel the vibration of harmony of all life that is at the very center of our being. Years ago in comic strips (and more recently on *Star Trek*) you would see meters that supposedly read the vibration of life. Yes, we do have a bodily "vibratory" expression corresponding to what we're thinking and feeling.

In healing prayer, we don't create anything; we reveal and accept what already is: a living God that is expressing through us. So a normal attitude, a healthy attitude would be a total trust in God and, correspondingly, a trust in the authority of our word in the power of prayer. Note how as soon as we take the advice of a physician or a metaphysician, we feel free from depression, because we've changed our self-attitude. You may go in to the physician and feel "I've had it." The physician will say, "There, there; it's a minor thing; we can take care of it: just a couple of days in bed; rest; and take this three times a day" (even though it may be a placebo). And in the process you think, "Gee! It's not so bad," and immediately you begin to get better. And so attitudes make us feel well or sick. Your self-attitude determines the health of your body.

I remember someone asking me once, "Where can I find a doctor honest enough to tell me that nothing is wrong?" The only thing I could think of was to say (this was at the time of the Vietnam War), "Join the Army." Seriously, we can change the quality and structure of our body, our part of the world, by changing the quality and structure of our thoughts and beliefs. There's a way of happiness and there's a way of sorrow, there's a way of health and there's a way of sickness. The latter is the knowledge of this world and the other is the wisdom called the Christ in the Bible taken from the Greek word *Christos*, meaning "the anointed." Our body is the result of our thinking. Whatever it may show of health or disease is made by thinking, feeling, and desiring—because there is a law of thought. It is present and rules everywhere.

"It's done unto you as you believe." It was hard for me at first to accept this. God has been good to me: He gave me a healthy body that repairs and renews itself through all kinds of pressures. So it was hard for me to understand—until it demonstrated itself several times in my life. But everything on the physical plane *is* an externalization of thought, because our minds are magnets that draw things to us. We're always attracting or repelling something. It is impossible to escape the law of cause and effect; and a thought creates either happy or unhappy experiences, either sickness or the health that we are born with. In business, thought decides whether it's a successful business.

The thing we must always understand in our healing prayer is that we're not trying to manipulate something, we're not trying to play God. In our healing prayer we're trying to reveal the inherently perfect, harmonious spirit of God, knowing that as that flows through the vehicle of our expression, wonderful things take place. Of course, many people don't like to accept this idea, for it places great responsibility on the individual. It's much easier to blame every event as circumstantial or the will of God. We have a mind; we think. We have a brain—three pounds of protoplasm—but there is something moving through that brain, using it as a computer. The brain does not think by itself; and so we say that the Mind of God, moving through us, is the source of all Power.

I had an old car for years, finally retiring it with close to 300,000 miles. The last year, I had to doctor that car so much that it cost more than when I bought it. Finally, in an act of understanding, I blessed it, released it, said goodbye to it, and donated it to the Portland School System, for use in their training workshops. Now I know they will rebuild it. It will have a new life. Everything will be perfect within it because they're working from the idea of what the car would be like if it were perfect. You could say it will be "healed"—healed of all its troubles, healed of all its "sins." A sin is a missing of the mark. It destroys cars, it destroys health.

Ernest Holmes said something years ago that attracted me to this teaching: "There is no sin but a mistake, there is no punishment but a consequence." And so I began to think that destructive thoughts are sin and constructive thoughts are not. Jesus took away mistakes, without attempting to moralize, because that was to deprive people of choice. He didn't try to put good in them; he knew it was already there. He said, "Be ye therefore perfect as your Father in Heaven is perfect," and that's the way our healing prayer works: we uncover in our healing prayers what is already there.

It's a new concept to say God is not sick—and neither am I. It's a new concept no matter how many thousands of years old the idea of it is. It's a new concept to say God is not poor, God is not unhappy—and neither am I. It's a new concept to say God is never confused, never out of place—and neither am I. This is how we base our healing prayers, and it seems so very simple an idea. Anything that created this world, this earth, and this universe in which we live is Itself in a balance of harmony and perfection. Therefore, anything emanating from this creation would have that perfection distilled within it, and even every gene would have that idea. Our healing is based on the idea that there's a spiritual you that is never sick, never afraid. Browning called it "the spark which man may desecrate but cannot quite lose." These are the tools of thought that we work with in this teaching; and we do it within ourselves.

We go to the doctor, to the hospital, to the psychologist in order to relieve the stress of the *effect*—of the *symptoms*—we're experiencing. We don't deny them; but we now reestablish the idea of wholeness. Even if we can find various roots—we say, for example, such-and-such is because of the way we were brought up, etc. The *past* was once a *future* that became a *present*. The only way it can affect us is if we accept it. So we in our work, as we pray, free our minds from past mistakes. We free our minds from negative threats. Healing prayer is the desire of every individual, in which it's *not* up to us to create a perfect God or a perfect being or a perfect man or a perfect body. Healing is a revelation or recognition that these already exist. God is; came; stayed; and isn't going anywhere.

When I attended Military School, every Sunday we were served chicken, mashed potatoes, and a sort of sickly yellow gravy poured over the top of the whole thing. When you got finished eating, if you left your plate for a couple of minutes you found that this yellow gravy (or whatever it was) had congealed and obscured the crest of the Military School, which appeared on the bottom of the plate. When the plate was removed to the kitchen and washed in hot water, the obscurity—the gravy— was removed, the plate was clean, and there was the pattern revealing itself. And so it is with us. In our healing prayer we scrape the gravy off the pattern.

The Wayshower, Jesus, said we go into the Secret Place to commune with the Father. And Dr. Alexis Carrel, the famous

French surgeon and biologist, said that "Prayer should be understood not as a mere mechanical recitation of formulas but as mystical elevation in the contemplation of a principle transcending our world." That's what we do in healing prayer. And it's done unto us as we believe. Therefore, the whole thing comes back to our belief. It's a conscious work we do on our belief. Whether we do it silently or speak it out loud: *believing*, we separate the condition and reveal what necessarily means so much to us—the wholeness, the perfection.

Happiness from Within

WE OFTEN HEAR that joy comes from within; success comes from within; peace comes from within; happiness comes from within. We know that we accomplish little by manipulating outer circumstances or trying to change other people. We work on ourselves; we pray; and always our inner joy, our inner serenity, precedes the peace that reflects itself into our outer world.

Every teaching has a gospel. Ours has no tenets and no dogmas, no doctrines, no superstitions, and no fears. Yet we do have one thing that's consistent—sort of a new gospel, if you will—and that gospel is the power within you, the joy that we can temporarily hide but really never extinguish.

The Law of God expressing through the sheer joy and happiness within us is the delight of our creative manifestation in our world. The "secret" of this is really no secret at all. In fact, we teach only three things: we teach that there's one God common unto all of us. We teach that there's something that responds to our thought. And we teach the Eleventh Commandment: "Thou shalt love one another as I have loved you."

So the question seems to me to be a matter of choice: do we

choose to stay angered with the anxieties, the fears, the tensions, saying, "Oh! What a terrible world it is we live in!" Or do we choose to say, "I'm just going to let go and let that bubbling wellspring of God's infinite Love move through me into everything I'm doing." Are we going to say, by choice, that we will wait no longer for other people to perfectly embody that happiness and serenity? And are we going to add, "I will begin now to build the foundation for serenity within myself"?

We get so caught up in all our "stuff" that we don't see clearly. This is like the story of the little girl who didn't dust the furniture to suit her grandmother. Her grandmother made her do it again and again, and still she wasn't satisfied. Finally the little girl, with a twinkle in her eye, said, "Grandmother, that dust isn't on the furniture; *it's on your glasses!*"

To have a cheerful heart we have to begin to make friends with ourselves. We have to be able to say, "I love myself." We have to be able to say, "I feel great, and I want everyone in my life to feel as I do." How happy *are* we? Are we content? Are we secure? Do we really believe in God? Because if we do, we're secure in the joy and the happiness and the delight of all creation.

We can think and create and bring about, by our thoughts, anything we choose to in our life. Why would we choose the gloomy, the miserable, the sad, when for the pure joy and spontaneous delight of God bubbling through us, we can do the opposite? I think the only gauge is, are you more cheerful today than you were this same day a year ago? And it takes a lot of courage to answer that one. Because it takes a lot of courage just to be cheerful!

This reminds me of something I read in one of Norman Vincent Peale's little booklets—a true account of a woman with a very cheerful heart. She had had her eye removed. They were going to put a false eye in its place—she didn't want to wear a patch—and she made sure that the eye was fashioned with a twinkle in it. That takes a lot of courage.

It may take courage not to do some things, but in the main it's doing *better* things that leads to happiness and cheer. If nothing else, we can at least walk along the street and be cheerful, say, "Thank you, God; I can walk, I can talk, I can smile." Better than the old lament:

> I never cut my neighbor's throat.
> My neighbor's gold I never stole.
> I never cursed nor house nor land.
> But God have mercy on my soul
> For I am haunted night and day
> By deeds I have not done.
> Oh, unattempted loveliness!
> Oh, costly battle never won!

I used to travel around the country with my wife, Ann. We were lecturing on our books, having fun, enjoying it all—and we found that wherever we went, even coming into a strange town and walking through the hotel lobby or on the street, if we smiled, people smiled back at us. It's contagious. All that's needed is the awareness that we are magnificent living, loving, joyous, creative expressions of God with the power to co-create that joy into everything in our life.

This, then, produces the happiness that we think about so longingly. And this happiness is distinguished from mere pleasure. We can all run away from the cares of the world, say, "I'm going to a party," "I'm going to forget it all." We imbibe too much or we stay up too late, and the next morning we're right back where we started from. That's pleasure. The source of pleasure can end, but the joy in our heart can never end—because it's a state of mental awareness.

I find that a lot of our problems stem from our resenting happiness in others. I remember someone once came in laughing, singing, and whistling—and I said, "How disgusting, so early in the morning!" (I had been to a party the night before.) I've also found that most of why we're so grumpy with other people is because we're trying to change them and they're trying to change us. Little wonder if we're confused.

I, for one, confess to being confused. I'm confused about everybody talking about God and yet not expressing God in their lives. I know that all humankind is good, and yet all I hear is how terrible humankind is. There's no answer this way. Only when we *accept* are we God in expression. How can we think the way we do if we are feeling the song of the Universe? And there *is* a song. In the sound of the seashell that you pick up at the shore and put to your ear—there is more—much more—than the sound of the tide going in and out. You hear the breath of God inhaling and exhaling. You hear a vibration, an energy—and remember: thought is energy, and all energy is motion. So if you're thinking joyously with a cheerful heart, that vibration will transform everything, like the alchemy of changing lead into gold.

We argue that our teaching can't give us a cheerful heart. "What has God to do with a cheerful heart?" As Ernest Holmes said, we throw the baby out with the bath water. He taught a happy teaching. Jesus taught a happy teaching. A teaching that says you don't have to suffer. You don't have to be miserable. Laugh; feel the joy and delight of God.

Each one of us is going to express the joy of God in a different way. Some will overcome an affliction and feel joyous and happy because they've overcome the affliction and they're giving something to the world. Some will feel joy because they can sing, they can play music, they can express themselves. Some others because they can transcend all kinds of things taking place in their lives. Still others when they are baking or cooking for other people. We shall all express it in a different way.

The best thing is that we stop *trying* to be cheerful. Have you noticed, sometimes, on television those plastic grins? The first thing you think is "I wonder how many facelifts they've had, because if they grin any wider, their faces will crack."

If we see the genuine joy and the happiness in another, it's because we're happy inside of ourselves. We don't *try* to be happy; we're happy in what we *do*. This doesn't imply that we're perfect. I'm not perfect. I don't know how anybody can put up with a minister working around the clock. It is more than I can understand. Yet my wife gives me a lot of happiness and does a lot of things for me. I'm stubborn, obstinate sometimes. Yet I do have one or two good qualities. It's like perfume: a good scent intended for others comes wafted back to you.

A lot of people say, "You ministers live in an unreal world. You bounce around with 'Whee! God is love! Isn't it great??' You can't be serious! You're not that way all the time! That's a dream, an illusion."

But you and I know it's not an illusion. We have searched for something and we have variously found it. We have transcended the symptom that somebody had labeled as cancer. We have transcended the lack of work and creative expression. We have transcended the inability to see, with eyes opened so that we *could* see. We number among us all of these people—and more. I've always said that if you expose yourself just three times to the principles formulated by Ernest Holmes, you can never get away from them. You may in disgust go back to where you came from—but you'll never be comfortable, because the joy won't be there.

We need to get rid of old, dead ideas. Get new fresh thoughts right now. Take all the other thoughts and put them somewhere—burn them—give them away—and say, "I'm happy that I can feel," and say, "I am God in joyous expression. I am an extension, an expression of all the joy and harmony there is in the world." That's what we need to do. A song in our hearts, a song in our heads, a song of recognition that we are the sun, the moon, the stars, the flight of the bird, the laughter of the child, the sound of the music. *That's* the cheerful heart.

Let's see happiness. As the world-famous singer Jenny Lind always said at the conclusion of her 20 minutes alone in a private room every night before her performance: "Let me ring true tonight." That's love—if we have great joy in our life and if we allow it to come through. Then all heaviness and burden falls away, and that spontaneous Thing flushes through us, circulating, cleaning out anything unlike the joyous nature of all Creation.

A Change for the Better

EVERY TIME I'M with a group of people dedicated to our teaching, I feel that we ought to be very happy that we know the things we know—and we do know quite a lot. At the same time, I sometimes think we ought to be sad—that we don't do more about it. We have a combination of all of the teachings of the great and the wise put together by Ernest Holmes, catalyzing it all into one teaching. It is not a dogma; it has no superstition, no fear. But Dr. Holmes sometimes said that we focus so much on the teaching, we forget to practice it. Indeed, we may have a timidity about it.

I know we feel that the teaching has made our lives beautiful; but I sometimes wonder if we haven't questioned how it happened—because perhaps we don't understand it. Other times, I wonder if we believe it and even understand it, but don't embody it in our daily activities. Sometimes, though, we need to stop questioning and accept its action—because we don't want merely to take an old, worn-out experience or habit and make something new out of it. We believe, rather, that we can institute *a whole new direction* and *a wholly new way of thinking*.

But sometimes *a new fear* comes in: "What will I do?"
"How will I handle it?" "Will I be able to work with it?" Somehow it reminds me of the man who said, "I have insomnia so
bad I can't even sleep when it's time to get up!" Isn't that aw-
ful? It's certainly not the happiness that comes from the pure joy
of being, from the joy of living, from the joy of knowing that we
can do something to create a new way of life for us.

Strangely enough, there are those that think they could be
happy without cares or responsibility. Some people pray to be
released from it. This reminds me of the former prison inmate
who told me, "You know, it was very calm, it was very nice,
it was very peaceful in there." No one can find happiness who
can't achieve victory over the "invitations" extended by the
crises in their lives.

I think half of the mistakes we make in our life derive from
feeling when we ought to *think*, and *thinking* when we ought
to *feel*. But we've got to arrive at some sort of a balance. One
of the virtues of being very young is that you don't let the facts
get in the way of your imagination, and so it's a lot easier to be
happy. But even the very young can be vulnerable, as witness
this from *Readers Digest:*

> My cousin's wife, a third-grade teacher, told her class one
> day, "Any citizen of the U.S. can become President."
> One boy with a strong interest in history and politics
> asked if even *he* could be President. After she assured
> him he was eligible, he thought it over and asked, "What
> if the Cabinet finds out I can't tie my shoes?"

The thing that often prevents us from moving in that new
direction is a kind of apathy. "Why should I try?" "What's going to happen? Nothing is going to happen." "Where is God?
He's not in *my* life!" I saw a slogan once that said, "Apathy is
our most serious problem." Underneath it was: "But who
cares?" But there isn't room for apathy in the Power of God

Within. And I don't mean *within someone else*. I mean the Power in *you*. The power to pray, in particular.

Prayer is a *very* powerful energy, an energy that crosses areas of darkness and reaches into every corner of the world. The Psalmist affirmed—and these are the words that Jesus and the disciples sang as they marched up the hill into the city on Palm Sunday—"I will lift up mine eyes unto the hills from whence cometh my help." We are saying—and doing—the same thing in Spiritual Mind Treatment.

In our teaching we have a tendency to tell and to listen to a lot of success stories. We are people who look and act healthy, exuding confidence. That's the kind of thing we love. But the first-timer looks in and is troubled. He sees all this exuding and vibration of energy, and he says, "Gosh, that's depressing! How *do* those people do it? They talk about prayer, they talk about a thing called Spiritual Mind Treatment, and they don't seem to have any problems—only minor challenges. Their supply is assured and abundant, their cup runneth over. The divine Power within them is always working—computing, creating, healing, loving, and blessing. I want to know: how *did* they get that way?"

You get that way by recognizing that there are no exceptions: *each individual* has the right to grow, love, and be happy. But most of us make our progress the hard way. Still, there really is no easy way in our teaching, even though it is the simplest teaching in the world. In fact it's very difficult, because it says that you have to do it yourself, step by step. After a while, there are no crises—just opportunities. Basically, opportunities to *believe*.

I have always felt that any religion, any religious belief, any denomination should allow each individual the opportunity of being happy. Some of us remember from early days in religion that you had to tiptoe into the church. If you spoke above a whisper, it was as though the crystal in God's china closet would break. You had to sit down, never laugh, but look very somber and pious. This can become ingrained within us.

Instead, I've always felt that all creation and all humankind exists for the delight of God. And the delight of God is a simple, straightforward thing. Did you know that the story of creation is written in 400 words? The Declaration of Independence has 1821 words. And one of our government's publications, on a reduction in the price of cat food, takes up 2500 words. *More and more about less and less.*

The *delight* of God: the *happiness* of God. How happy are *you? Deliriously* happy? *Quietly* happy? Are you contented? Secure? The happiness that we speak of is really the Power of the Living God within us, and through that Power we are sustained and maintained—whether we need to do something or stop doing something; whether we need to know something or just get clear on something we think we know that just isn't so; whether we need the healing power of God's love in our lives; whether we need a positive goal; whether we need the things that will benefit ourselves and our family; whether we need the confidence to look forward as we move in a new direction of change; whether we need to recognize our possibilities and to have the inner strength so that we can say Yes or No. *The Power works through you.*

A small boy lowered his head at the dinner table one evening and told his parents that there was to be a small PTA meeting the next day. "Well, if it's just a small one, do you think we ought to go?" asked the parents. "I'm afraid so," said the youngster. "It's just you, me, and the principal." And that's what our teaching is. You, me, and the principles of right living and happiness. And already we have these principles established within ourselves.

We believe, because we are Christians and more, in the teaching of the Great Wayshower. We believe it when he says always to treat others as you want them to treat you: "And whatsoever ye would that men do to you, do ye also unto them." I've always thought: he doesn't say, "Wouldn't it be *nice* if you did this?" or "Make life easier for yourself!" He *did* say, "This is the Law and the Prophets."

I used to read a lot of Harry Emerson Fosdick, the pastor of New York's famed Riverside Church—a huge institution. He was for many years a noted religious leader. One day, when Harry Emerson was still a boy, his father called back from the front gate of their house to Mrs. Fosdick, "Tell Harry if he wants, he can cut the grass when he gets home from school." Harry smiled, because he had already made his choice. But then came his father's further words: "And tell Harry he'd better want to."

Our own true spiritual reflection is one of perfection, for we are created in the image of the Heavenly Father, and it is only when this image is modified by doubt, anxiety, and underestimation that the reflection becomes distorted and blurred. But we have the power to institute a new way; we have the power to select direction—the shape and the form we want our life to take. Do we *know* the direction we want our life to take? Yet it *can* be fulfilled, because we have been given the gift of choice, the "Pearl of great Price." If we are asked, "Who is in charge here?" shall we answer and say, "My problems, my doubts, my fears, my worries," or will it be "*I* am; I and the Loving Father. For I choose to direct the Power of God within towards peace, harmony, and hope."

Our teaching offers us the opportunity of enlarging, enriching, and fulfilling our lives in a private place within us that is very personal and sacred—a room within that we can enter and where we can establish a communion and feel a Presence, a sense of the drift of the heavens themselves. And as we stand in that personal room, we know that we are a part of everyone else. For our room is the same as the room of every other one, no matter what the outer appearance may be. Then in this feeling, this recognition, putting aside the form of appearances and the judgments we've made, we can feel a great love, a great, serene feeling of peace and harmony, and we can know that it envelopes everyone in the world, even those engaged in conflicts; that peace and love enfold them.

And as we return to the world of experiences, we can become aware of an energy, one that perhaps we've overlooked before—the energy of a silent voice that says, "Lo, I am always with you"; the energy that says, "Every part of your body and being is of Me," that every part of your life is of Mind. And as this becomes our word, we are healed and restored and renewed.

The Anatomy of Prayer

THE ANATOMY OF PRAYER is a subject that ought to be of most vital interest to all of us.* In this connection, one of the mistakes we most commonly make is in the very idea of *why* we pray. I think that most of us pray to materialize something, to get something. It seems that 80 percent of the time I'm listening to people talking about their needs. Most of us forget that prayer is the opening of a window in our individual consciousness—that prayer enables us, with faith and confidence, to surrender an old belief or an old idea, leaving us open to a redirection of the creative energy, the power of thought, through us in whatever way enables us to move forward.

I think prayer should never be thought of as just informing God of our individual needs. I remember Jesus' words, Your Father knows what you have need of. I believe that as we release this idea, we get a greater ability to pray. For example, there may be some particular experience or situation that seemingly is

* A favorite subject of Doctor Bendall's, it figures most prominently in the title of his second volume of *The Holmes Papers: The Anatomy of Healing Prayer*—talks given by Ernest Holmes and compiled by Doctor Bendall.

71

stuck. We can't release it. The idea of prayer, then is for us to cut the bondage. Because the only reason we're holding on to it is fear that there is a God or a Universe that will give us something else, and we won't be able to handle it. So when we're praying properly, we're effecting a *release*—because the motive of all life is for us to keep moving; to have new experiences, new challenges; to be able to conquer them and pass on to others to clear our minds and have new things flow through us and be a part of us.

I recall the story of the man who was making the great transition and someone said, "Henry, have you made your peace with God?" He answered, "I'm not aware that we had ever quarreled." You and I too must be in such a position that we can rid ourselves of the notion that we've been on the outs with God. I've had people say, "I don't think God heard me." "I don't think God knows that I'm here." "It must be because I've sinned." The idea of prayer is to clear this kind of sediment from our spiritual and mental life.

We turn to prayer because somewhere the stream is not flowing as it should. It's like a pipe that breaks in the middle, so that there's no water coming through. The idea of prayer is to reconnect those two pieces of pipe so that the water can resume its flow through them. We might say that one end of the pipe is "universal" pipe, the main pipeline, indestructible, stable, secure—with always something flowing through it. The other is the individual. This is "flexible" pipe, because it has the power to twist this way and that—with sometimes the happy knack of untwisting from the slow stream and becoming aligned with the "universal" pipe and its life-giving water, which we all seek.

Prayer enables us to untwist. It clears the sediment from our lives. But it also rids us of the idea that God is the Super Fixer. If anything has diminished the purity of our teaching, it's the idea that God is a great Super Fixer like some kind of Mend-All

Kit or All-Purpose Glue that holds everything together, and all you've got to do is squirt it out of the tube. Nothing could be further from the truth than this notion that God is some sort of cosmic Errand Boy to be summoned whenever anything needs fetching. We must accept the idea that prayer is a release.

Some years ago in New York City there was the "scandal" of the Collier brothers—two millionaire recluses who inhabited a mansion stuffed to the rafters with newspapers, furniture, canned goods, and all kinds of junk. You couldn't walk through the house. There wasn't room to add anything else, it was so stuffed with things. How healthful it would instead have been to have it opened up, exposed and airy, with the circulation of life flowing through—the idea of releasing, and of taking on new things.

Prayer as Jesus taught it when he said, "Pick up your bed and walk," is to give us the privilege of the greatest life benefit that we have: not the privilege of sitting and being without a problem but the privilege of living and knowing that life flows through us with all of its dynamic qualities, enabling us to meet the challenges to grow emotionally and mentally, and not to submit to the boring consistency of a dull complacency in which, whenever something gets out of order, we summon the Super Fixer.

I think we've seen a tremendous amount of this. It's amazing to me, in a teaching as free from fear as ours is, to see how many old ideas of prayer keep hanging on. In talking with a very prominent personality in our movement some years ago, I suggested that he give the closing meditation. And the meditation was filled with "I shall," "tomorrow," "it will," etc.—with futurity and no expectation of *the now*. But the important thing is that *now* is when prayer clears the sediment and lets the new experience enter in. And this becomes our story—the story of a life everlasting. We move from one experience into another with confidence and security. So whenever the period of time comes for us to move from this experience to another, we move with confidence and security into it. This is what is meant by eternal life.

Often, however, we're just pleading—even though we're rephrasing it in terms of Religious Science—before a capricious God, one who may grant our desires if we grovel enough. We have to rid ourselves of the old ideas of prayer connected with sin and the practices of people. We don't have to agree with them. If they play cards, that's their privilege. If they go dancing, it's also their privilege. (I leave the other things to your imagination.) It's every individual's privilege—and responsibility. How many times do we pray in judgment even for ourselves? We pray *condemning ourselves in the framework of the prayer* and then say, "Now, God, take this away from me." But we've already established it.

Two shipwrecked men were afloat on a raft. After they had been there about fifteen days, one of them said, "O God, if You will only save me I'll be the best man in the world. I'll go to church every Sunday. I'll never swear or steal again. I'll always treat my wife with respect." And he went on and on. The other fellow suddenly raised himself on his elbow and said, "Wait! Before you go on: I think I see a sail!"

You see, we need to pray with a greater sincerity. We need to recognize that prayer is about loosening, rendering, and establishing in our lives a fresh experience greater than the one before it, with the definite desire to situate ourselves in peace and harmony. We need to recognize that we don't necessarily have to meditate in language, affirmations, and the use of Religious Science terms in order to pray. We can pray in our thought and by the purity of our own understanding.

I think we do need to remember, though, that we've got a mind, a mentality—something that can think and say, "I'm going to sit down, learn, and apply this teaching." Because we've got a body that will obey the mind and sit down! And we've got the necessary environment, which is also a part of us, the product of our use of mind. And yet, with all of this going for us, what do we do? We scramble across the face of the earth, digging, clawing, pushing, kicking, biting. Yet our whole function is to express the creative life to the fullest degree possible with the dignity of work, with the dignity of touching other people, as we move in prayer from the surrender of one old idea to another, new, one.

We discover one law of nature after another. And the more we discover, the greater the experience. Of course, all the philosophers of all time have said this; and we can think in the same way. What's unfortunate is the things we *do* think about. And yet we know that the condition of our thought determines the thing. If only we would let ourselves flow with the flow of life! For example, suppose I asked you to give me a one-line affirmation, and you came up with what you thought was an affirmation. But it might also *not* be an affirmation, depending upon the conviction of your belief. You can see how holding on to all the old experiences is not going to work.

There are so many times, then, that prayer is not answered because there has been a violation of the fundamental principle to surrender the old ideas and let the new ones in. Unless we change our thinking, there's no use in praying, and we're just wasting our time. We're not here to collect more stuff. That's worthless. We *are* here to learn to expand ourselves, to surrender old ideas, to surrender old experiences, to take new ones in with confidence. This is why we have to pray—so we can turn to something and say, ''I know that I can face this new challenge without fear; and once I handle it, I know there'll be a bigger one behind it.''

One of our big problems is the habits that we set up. A habit can be a very good thing. We need habits for protection. We need habits of thinking—although once we've conditioned the sub-conscious (in a cold way of speaking), our work is nothing but the repetition of an idea from the conscious mind. And in just this way we may also establish ourselves in ruts—even if they're sometimes automatic habit patterns for the good. But the difficulty is that we can get into a destructive form of prayer and create a habit pattern that makes it a continual loser, where we even find ourselves saying, "My prayers are never answered; I never get a thing." But you know that our prayer *was* answered. We prayed knowing we were never going to get anything, so we got an abundance of nothing. This is the thing that we need to recognize. The difference is between being "evangelical"—"I'm a winner with God this morning"—and the customary assumption, "I'm a loser."

We have lost nothing. We can only "lose" that which isn't ours to lose in the first place. Besides, the so-called loser has the advantage, actually; because if you beat me in a game of checkers, say, the challenge to me is to some day beat you. You may beat me seven times, but perhaps you play the same old game, and you become complacent in a rut of thinking; whereas I am trying, not just for the sake of beating you, to win and pass on to greater ability.

If we're repeating the same mistakes and getting nowhere, we're in a rut. And the very power of prayer that we seek to use affirmatively is then sapping us, draining us, keeping us in this rut. But there's a beautiful part of all this: whatever designing Intelligence, whatever caring God created us, the image of His own thinking, established us, giving us the grace of redirection of the creative energy, and as much as said, "I've given you something, but you'll have to find it: I've given you the ability to create and to be a part of my creative Universe." We're a bundle of habits. If we're a bundle of habits in the physical world, we're a bundle of habits in the prayer.

If you have a problem praying—if you're praying and not getting anywhere—look in a mirror, look at yourself, and break the pattern of it. Perhaps you know the expression "Oh, he's just as comfortable as an old shoe to be with.'' That refers to the ''habit'' of the leather to become set to the foot. How many old shoes have you got in your prayer closet? How many old shoes have you got there?

It's well to realize that prayer is a natural, and not unnatural, function. Nor is it something *supplementary*. We pray all the time; every thought is a prayer—and as we believe, so it is. And when we talk about prayer we're talking not about a process of asking for something—asking some being or God to function for us. We are talking about learning an art: the art of selective seeing.

Jesus looked at the world and saw what he wanted to see. He had learned this art. As a result, he was able to project his vision of reality, and what he believed became real. He saw the perfect person and knew that it was not necessary for us to suffer or to be sick or in bondage in order to be Godlike. To be Godlike was to be perfect. He taught praising and blessing and thanking God —thanking God because of the perfection that he knew was already here. This selective seeing can be our new habit, yielding new results and a new life. It can be, and *should* be, our anatomy of prayer.

It's a Sin to Be Poor

YEARS AGO ERNEST HOLMES said to me, "George, there is nothing that degrades our teaching more than to think it is a get-rich-quick scheme where we can come in and demonstrate piles of dollars up to the ceiling and immediately have Rolls Royces and castles on the Rhine, sailboats and yachts; because," he said, "it is *not* a get-rich-quick scheme. But," he added, "there should be no one in the teaching that is ever without anything."

I discussed this with another gentleman, an old teacher of mine by the name of Dr. Paul Martin Brunet,* author of the book *Master Meditations*. The very first time I talked with Paul, he said, "You know, the deadliest sin of all is *the sin of being poor*."

We know that richness comes from a wealth of abundant mental attitudes. One Wednesday evening in the practitioner training class, we all got together in a treatment for unexpected

---

* Paul Martin Brunet was a pioneer of Religious Science in New York City, founder of Second Church and Institute of Religious Science.

good, and as a result of it quite a few in the group experienced that good. So it's a matter of thinking. Each one here, within the possibility of their realization, should be able to have whatever it is they want.

Now it's a great mistake to say, "*Take what you wish,* for you can have anything you like." We don't take what we wish, but *we attract to us what is like our thoughts.* That is in keeping with our teaching. We must *become* more if we wish to draw a greater good into our life. And as we recognize the storehouse of the Universe and the abundance of it, we draw abundance to us.

I remember a line made famous by the late famous singer (I'm probably dating myself) Sophie Tucker, who said, "I've been rich and I've been poor, but believe me, rich is much better!" I agree with it, and if we are honest with ourselves, we can agree that it *is* right for us, in the framework of our teaching, to live graciously and abundantly, to have our bills paid, to have more than enough to meet our needs, to know that if we want something—for example, a new suit or a new dress or a car—that we have the means for it.

But let's understand that I'm not just talking about *money* when I say it's a sin to be poor. I'm talking about the *consciousness of abundance,* that which completely eliminates even the very *idea* of being poor. Now there is really only one Law in the Universe, which is what we are dealing with. And a very definite aspect of this in our Science of Mind teaching is the law of multiplication. We multiply an idea many times over until it comes forth. We have the idea, and it multiples and multiplies and multiplies.

In fact, that's what happens when we have what we call a *demonstration.* We sit down and say, "This is what I want to demonstrate." We multiply the idea, and from that multiplication the demonstration comes into being. The abundance, the richness of our life, is the multiplication of the idea that it's right for us to have it, that it's right for us to be able to live comfortably and graciously.

Everyone has a desire for this; but sometimes it seems that other people are having greener grass, and we say, "Why should *they* have it? Look at how stupid they are!" But: they have an *abundance* consciousness. Most of the people with whom I have ever talked who had great wealth were not conscious that they had wealth or possessions. They just had a sense that "It's *right* for me to have this . . . it's right for me to have this abundance."

You know some of the clichés: if someone pursues money, we say they're *money-mad*. If someone holds on to it, we say they're *cheap*, they're capitalists. If someone spends seemingly more than they should, we call them *frivolous* and *playboys* or *playgirls*. If someone doesn't have it, we say look how *worthless* they are. If someone doesn't try, we say they don't have any *ambition*. If someone accumulates a lot of it, we say it's a *fool* who got *lucky*. But none of these are what we are talking about. We're talking about "*It's a sin to be poor.*" And we know that all sin is *a missing of the mark*.

Now everything that I have ever read has always indicated that the Kingdom of Heaven is open to us. "Abundance is thine, saith the Lord." "I have meat to eat, that you know not of." It's *there*, and we, in our teaching, should have this as one of its primary features—that the world, the Universe, the Mind of God that we are using individually is open not to limitation, but to the abundance of all good things: an abundance of love, an abundance of happiness, an abundance of joy, an abundance of beauty, an abundance of health . . . most importantly, an abundance of health. But you see, *abundance* covers it all. We are just as poor if we are poor in health and have worldly goods as we are if we don't have any worldly goods.

"Abundance is thine." I think if I were to define it, I would say it is *the ability to love, to be loved, to be happy, to do the things that we want to do at the time we want to do them—the ability to have a wealth of creative ideas and creative thoughts, the ability to have a wealth of friends and people that you love and that love you.* Abundance is a part of the living—and should be—of every person in this teaching.

"To him who believes, it shall be done." It's a *knowingness* that's able to stand in front of a conditioned world and project, if you will, an unformed idea into that world and multiply it abundantly. You see, we spend so much time in praying and treating to get something we haven't got, that by the very fact of our praying to get what we haven't got, we're giving power to *what we haven't got.* Yet "to them that *have* shall be *given;* and from them that have *not,* even that which they have shall be *taken from them.*" I've quoted this scripture before, and it's still the only appropriate saying that fits the situation.

Think of how many times you pray to get something. The minute you do this, you are saying that *you don't have it.* And the teaching says, not unrealistically, For heaven's sake, don't write checks on the Bank of God and expect God to cover them when they hit the bank. I had someone do that one time. It just doesn't work that way.

However, with the abundant *consciousness,* wherever you go there *is* an abundance of everything. There is an abundance of flowers in your garden. There is an abundance of peace and love and happiness. There is an abundance of the good things in life. So with this consciousness we can brave a world that's scrambling, scratching, struggling, driving, to *collect*—including the Internal Revenue Service. I even found myself uttering a few choice words about that bunch—and then I began to think: If I hadn't gotten anything, I wouldn't have been able to utter the few choice words!

As you give, you receive. And with an *abundance* of giving-ness, we know, according to our teaching, that there is no void that will not be filled. Let me give you an example. In Palestine, there are two seas. There is the Sea of Galilee, whose shores Jesus walked along, which is fresh water. It has fish and green foliage. Children play alongside it—or did. The water comes from the hills and is good to drink. Life abounds—truly, an *abundant* situation.

But the Sea of Galilee flows on south into another sea, which has been labeled the Dead Sea. It's the same water—but there's no fish in it, no life, and neither man nor beast will drink it. The River Jordan flows into both of these seas. The Sea of Galilee *receives* and *gives it out*, and as such it continues to receive the fresh water, the *abundance* of that water from the mountains. It *gives*, and it *lives*. The Dead Sea? It gives nothing and dies.

You see, "abundance—in order to receive it, we give it" wasn't just invented by ministers for collections; it's a good idea. As you give it, it comes back to you—*abundantly*. It *gives* and it *lives*. That which does not have the abundance consciousness *gives* nothing, *receives* nothing, and dies.

Now this law of multiplication, which is the cornerstone of our teaching, implies the increase of something that *already* exists. We can't get it unless it is *already there*. What this implies is that it is *increasing* itself and giving *more* and *more*. But we have to recognize it within ourselves and apply it. We have to believe it.

Now we believe—and Ernest Holmes always definitely believed—that the dynamic principle of life is not death-oriented, nor even survival-oriented, but *growth*-oriented. Our preoccupation with death puts us immediately on the track where we spend the rest of our time here racing to it. But our teaching believes that we are prepared to live, to be abundant here, today, and not get ready to die tomorrow. A continuity of life, love, and expression: *that's* abundance.

Our teaching is really the same as Jesus' own. Ernest Holmes used to say, "I never created anything new. I just took the best" —a doctrine of life, a doctrine of *use*. Then, as now, it was a sin to be poor. When they needed money to pay the taxes, Jesus said, "Oh, well, is that all you're fretting about? Throw a line in the water and pull out a fish and cut it open." And there was the coin. When they ran out of wine at the wedding feast, he said, "Pour the wine." He accepted the abundance. On another occasion, he called a kid over and said, "Hey, there's a law of abundance and it multiplies itself. What have you got in your bag?" The kid said, "I've got a couple of little fish, a hunk of bread, a piece of cheese." Jesus said, "Feed everybody."

Now you see, *what you use uses you*. If you use the *abundance* principle of the teaching, it uses you. But if you spend all your time using it to overcome what you *haven't got*, you're not going to get it, because you will always have to *overcome*, and the abundance principle is not there. The strange thing about the Universe, which only proves the principle, is that the Universe never says No. It says Yes. There aren't *two* laws—a law of being poor and a law of being abundant. That's why poverty is such a sin: because you're *abundantly* poor. And that's a terrible sin!

At some point along the line, we have to get back into the law of growth. But remember: that which you don't use *abuses* you, and you lose it. And that which you use, uses you well. So to grow spiritually, we need to nourish ourselves with this teaching. We need to sustain ourselves with the knowledge that it is true. And we need to know that wherever we go, our environment is that which reflects that feeling.

People say to me, "Where I go, they're always poor-mouthing." *Stay away from those places.* What should suit us for our environment is our abundant consciousness and practice of the teaching. A plant will die without sunshine and moisture; when the land is sour, it becomes dead. But when we breathe into them love and abundance, they multiply. Every plant in my office has emerged from a sick little weedling that people thought wouldn't flourish. But I talk to my plants. I bless them. I believe in that. And every plant, I am happy to report, is happy and doing well. (We've had to send a couple to the sick bay a couple of times because their consciousness wasn't right, but we got them back on the trail.)

Today, many of our "traditional" diseases have been removed: scurvy. Beriberi. Pellagra. They don't even exist any more. Measles are almost wiped out across the face of the earth. The plack plague, typhoid—all of these seem to be under control. But we worked at it. We nourished the idea of health and took all the steps to do it. It was a *sin* for the human race to be as poor in health as it was. Similarly, a mind without the proper nourishment sickens and becomes (not neurotic, because we're all happy, delightful neurotics!) really *psychotic*.

You can say what you want, but in treatment, in prayer, and in our teaching, *it's a sin to be poor*. Instead of condemning the things we don't have, we need to praise the things that we do have, knowing that they multiply themselves—because that which we have gets to be even more. If you don't use your imagination—if you haven't the consciousness of the abundance of that beauty, truth, and love—then it gets mixed up with rage, fear, lack, worry, and limitation. And we become a basket case.

The majority of the human race (and let's throw in the stock market) reflects that. Most of the wars that go on have an economic root. The dispute some years ago in the Falklands was because, even though both parties were ignoring it, there might be some oil around. The Civil War was started because the North couldn't compete with the cheap labor of the South in the textile mills. Always they had beautiful ideas—the ideological reasons why it all took place. But at the basis of it was greed. Somebody wanted what somebody else had.

We in our teaching don't have to want anything that anyone

else has. Some time ago, I listed the six things that Cicero said were the six mistakes of man: The delusion that personal gain is made by crushing others. The insistence on worrying about things that cannot be changed or corrected. Insisting a thing is impossible because you can't accomplish it. Refusing to set aside trivial preferences. Neglecting the development and refinement of the mind—and not acquiring the habit of reading and studying. Finally, attempting to make others live as we do. If we would heed those six points, of course we would have it all.

But you say, "How do we do it?" All right: we are always thinking and so we're always creating. So constructive thinking increases and expands. Destructive thinking decreases and deteriorates. Repetitive thinking, conforming to the way things are and have been, is boredom and we die from lack of use. So we might as well choose to think constructively.

We need to practice this teaching—to pray accepting our dominion and heritage. Practice thinking constructively. Take anything that you really have to do and that you've put off. List all of the ways you think it can be done. If you feel you have a limitation this morning, list all the ways you think you can get the abundance. List all the possible ways you can be prospered. God is unlimited, so why limit yourself?

List the things, the experiences, the friends, the people that you really want. Don't dream and set up illusions and fantasies. Be definite. Be clear. Examine your motives. Practice reversing all of the destructive ideas with the abundant, constructive ideas. List the beliefs you accept and the beliefs you reject, and analyze them. If the beliefs you accept include *limitation* and *being without* in any department of your life, then edit the list. Switch the unhealthy thoughts to the healthy thoughts that are your right.

Practice thinking what you *want* to think, not what someone thinks you *ought* to think—because they think *they* ought to think what *you* think you ought to be thinking about! Direct your thoughts to all the enjoyable, active things. Imagine new experiences, new reactions, new self-images. Limber up your thinking. Stiff thinking is just terrrible. It's a *sin*!

All this will be simple when you and I stop thinking it's hard. Everything in the Universe moves in circles, as when Jesus said, "Give, and unto you it shall be given; in good measure, well shaken down and running over, shall men press it into your hands." But we have to know that we stop pressing it when we don't believe in it. We have to know that we have an abundance of love to give to the world, and that we're not just *in* God, or *of* God, or *with* God—implying separation and division. We are an extension and expression of an abundant Universe, of an omnipotent Presence, the Presence of God. The joy of this idea is itself abundance.

The only "sin" in our teaching—and we don't believe in *sins*, because we don't sit in moral judgement (we never have and we never will; we morally police ourselves)—the only sin is to be *poor*. The only sin.

The following is based on a line from Lucan, the first-century Roman poet:

"How Blind Men Are to Heaven's Gifts"

The abundance of life, peace and security that we all desire surrounds us constantly. As we day by day realize the impossibility of God's containing any counterpart of limitation, we increase our abundance. Responding to the karmic law of cause and effect, we are the sum total of our thoughts and experiences. When we accept limitation as a personally imposed mental attitude, then we have taken the first step to abundance materially, spiritually, and physically.

I identify myself *now* with the infinite source of all supply.

I *know* that I am led, directed, and sustained by God.

I release any idea that God is punishing or imposing limitation upon my being or affairs.

I am expanding daily in wisdom, understanding, and acceptance of God's expression through me as an individual. These words *now* open all doors for my ever increasing abundance. I am divinely prospered in all ways of life.

And so it is.*

* Meditation 24 from Dr. Bendall's *Now the Time*.

Conviction of More

A NATION EXPRESSES ITSELF at the level of the conviction of its citizens. If we are thinking unrest, violence, disturbances, problems, then the nation reflects these. A church expresses itself according to the level of the conviction of the members of the church. A family expresses itself at the level of the conviction of the family members; and if we individually say, "I have a problem with this relationship," then we are establishing that conviction, and God's Law says, "OK, you have a problem. My blessings."

If we are experiencing limitation, we feel that that is what we're doomed to, and so with any conviction that manifests in our life. Our body language shows it. We bend over with anxieties, because we've got the weight of the world on our shoulders. If we're seeking employment or better creativity in our lives, we say, "Nothing is working; and that is all I can expect." That conviction is what manifests itself.

Scientists and doctors tell us that little tiny brainfolds store all the habit patterns of thinking and believing and experiences in our life. So we in effect accept what is stored there and say,

"Beyond this, I can go no further." And yet how did those brain-folds get there? We put them there. The Wayshower said, "It is done unto you as you believe." Whatever our beliefs are is what those brainfolds are throwing out without any problem. We don't have to worry about it; the whole thing functions au-tomatically.

But I've always believed—and Ernest Holmes always empha-sized this—that you and I have the right to not stop at that limi-tation. We're told there's an unlimited good that we can have. We're told that whatever we believe about the Spirit of Life within us, it gives us the right to have dominion over our affairs. So somewhere, somehow, we make a decision—and we make a decision not so much out of change for the merely *better*, nice as that is, but we make a decision to establish *a new habit pat-tern* and to establish *a new life*.

I can hear someone saying to me, "Well I tried that, and it didn't work for me. Oh, it worked all right for a couple of weeks; but then the same old thing happened again." You see, that little brainfold is still there. And just when we might have had two or three months' improvement or respite, we suddenly find our-selves in sticky circumstances, and the little brainfold says, "They want me again!" and we experience the same thing all over again.

Yet all of us seek something better. All of us at times say, "Is that all there is?* Do I just keep going on this way?" We all seek to express more, to have a conviction of more. It's a nor-mal human desire. Yet how happy are we as compared to this

---

* Dr. Bendall was probably recalling the title of the song made popular by his good friend, singer Peggy Lee. In her autobiography, *Miss Peggy Lee*, she writes: "Hardly a day goes by now that I don't talk with George. I would do that with Ernest [Holmes], and when he left us, George sort of took over . . . I suspect Ernest told him to watch over us. Ernest and George were really like two guardian angels. . . ." (p. 175, Berkley edition).

time a year ago? Have we reached a higher level of expression and fulfillment—or are we basically having the same worries, "Things are tough," "I'm depressed," "What's going to happen to me?" Are we content—or is it a false contentment? Are we stubborn and say that it is too much trouble to change? (Stubbornness does have one very positive feature: you'll always know what you're going to think tomorrow.)

Sure we're going to have occasions to *choose*. But they are not going to be crises; they are going to be things that we have to face, handle, and decide "I'm going to go up a little bit more." There are still going to be unanswered questions; there are still going to be some little worries; there are still going to be situations. But they will be only minor challenges. And whereas some people say, when they are finally convinced that their supply is assured, "God sustains me and I have more than enough to meet all my needs," that simply isn't enough. No, you have to go higher. Whatever your needs are today, *increase* them—and stay convinced. You have a right to.

There is a power of Life expressed in the Book of Genesis in the Bible: "I give you dominion over all things." But we employ all the rest of the Bible in trying to deny that. You see, we have a habit. We say that God is in everyone—the selfsame God. And we say there's a power of conviction in everyone—the selfsame power. But we forget to mention the God in *me, today*; the conviction in *me, today*. Instead, we're talking about everyone else.

Now, what we do: some of us will jump up and be instantaneous in our acceptance. Others of us will be each day increasing the depth of that little brainfold. In any case, we want to try and break our destructive patterns. For this, we have to accept with conviction that each day we are one notch higher in the good and acceptance and healing of everything in our life. We have to have the confidence to look forward, to recognize the possibilities unlimited.

There is no superior or inferior. There is no high or low. *You are the highest individual in the Mind of God* with all of the possibilities consequent upon acceptance of that. But I've never known anyone whose confidence level was increased who didn't get a little more than they had before—and then stop. Because even though we start on a higher level, and even though there is an automatic process, those little brainfolds are working, whether we consciously set them in motion or not.

Do you use your habit pattern—or do you let it use you? When it uses us, we can't establish that better life, because patterns run in a one-track channel. Whatever is already in there is all that's going to express itself. If you're in a rut, remember what the Bible says: "Repent ye; the Kingdom of God is at hand." *Repent* means *get out of the rut.* And we can establish a new track of direction according to our conviction.

Wherever you are physically, mentally, emotionally, take it one notch higher. And don't let the "facts" get in the way of what you have the possibility to be convinced of. The only problem with facts is that we forget which *facts* to keep and which "facts" to throw away, and so we say that it's all too much for us. We become apathetic, we don't feel like making much effort.

So let's open wide the doors of our understanding and know that we *can* establish a new direction: Who's in charge of my life? Who *is* in charge of *my* life!? Is there nothing the matter with me?—is it all the matter with other people? And is it *my* problems, *my* doubts, and *my* fears? Or will I instead affirm the powerful words that Jesus spoke: *I Am.* "I am what Thou art, Thou art what I Am."

I will choose to direct this power to create a better life of peace and harmony and hope. Only I can accept that I have the right to establish a higher conviction. And it is done unto me as I am convinced that I have this right.

Living Prosperity

IT'S FUNNY HOW WE so often feel that we have a right
to be happy and a right to do what we wish. We don't even question these; but when the subject turns to money, we start to
squirm and look askance as if somehow money were not to be
discussed—as though money belonged on another planet. Somewhere along the way we've lost the sense that money and en-
riched living are as naturally ours as are other life qualities.

According to Ernest Holmes, all the things in our lives were
once thoughts. If that's so, what are our thoughts about money?
Is it evil, unspiritual, too complicated, not meant for us perhaps?
These concepts are sure to keep money from us, just as clarity
about it and open-hearted acceptance of it as one of God's
natural blessings are sure to draw it into our lives. The consciousness of acceptance in regard to a desired outcome is necessary. So let us, then, plan and build a good money consciousness,
declaring money a great good and ourselves as marvelously capable of enjoying and handling it. Most of all, let us know that
abundant living is one of the gifts of the Spirit.

We are too prone to think of prosperity in terms of material things, and even though we protest and quote a lot of beautiful metaphysical language, in reality the fear of money (yes, *fear*) enters in and preys a great deal upon the lives of people. It's a known fact that when a nation doesn't live in the prosperity of rich mental attitudes, the nation itself becomes poor and debilitated, setting itself up for a dictator or ruler of some kind. In social life we know that when there is a lack of the prosperity attitudes of friendship and love, these also wither—for what you praise increases and grows, and what you curse withers. When we think well and treat our bodies well, they respond prosperously. Life itself, as we live it with zeal and enthusiasm, gives us back a prosperity of living.

But we're so very much inclined to measure prosperity in other ways. It's always associated with the abundance of money, which we need to function. But the two are connected. So am I willing to learn about the true, living prosperity—to do the things necessary to make it possible, and to remove it from its attendant fear? Am I willing to discard all the previous ideas of myself or—if it's a collective thing—the ideas we've all had? Am I willing to let my intellect be only a lever to remove the callous and to let me be sensitive to the real things of life and God?

Now the necessity isn't just for happiness and greatness to flow from life to you, but they've got to flow from you and all of us to life. I think it's a great mistake to cheapen our teaching by saying that it provides you the avenue to take what you want. Nothing degrades it more. "Take what you want, because you can have anything you like." These people forget that there's a price to be paid for every choice made. We don't *take what we wish*, but we do *attract that which is like the inner*—the thought. For always the outer corresponds to the inner. And if the outer is harmonious and loving and peaceful like the inner, then always there will be the feeling, the living of prosperity.

So we talk about prosperity, abundance—and again, we're

not talking about *money* and *things*. Rather, we're talking about the understanding—the *inner feeling* of abundance. An abundance of health, of love; an abundance of giving to one another. Over and over again the abundance of *understanding* produces all the things we need. At this point, someone says to me, "OK, that's nice; but what are you talking about, and how do you define this abundance?" Perhaps in the smallest degree of "understanding" we can say it's *having a little more than enough*. But we've got to remember: the abundance is of *life*. Do you enjoy the *living*, do you enjoy expressing it—that abundance of *life*, right up to the time we make the transition to a higher place of understanding—?

Perhaps you will recall the analogy I like to make in this context with the Sea of Galilee and the Dead Sea.* The two have the Jordan River for their source. The Sea of Galilee receives from it and gives it out; and as it does, it continues to receive from the Jordan. It gives and it lives. The Dead Sea takes everything that's given to it, but in return gives nothing and dies. The law of increase implies something that already exists. That something is the life of God. But we must first discover that it exists within us and then apply this law, giving away the life as we understand it.

Now in our teaching (and I call it Religious Science, but it's the Truth that has been taught by the great and wise for many years; Ernest Holmes always said, "I have created nothing new—I have only taken the best from all the teachings") the principle of life is not just to survive, but to grow. Ernest used to say, "We prepare you to live each day to the fullest, to accept life and give—not prepare you to die": a continuity of life, of love and expression.

This thinking derives from Jesus. His doctrine was not the doctrine of survival, but the doctrine of use. Our spine shows

* See p. 82.

evidence of a one-time tail; somewhere along the line we stopped tree climbing and we walked on the ground. And what you don't use, you lose. So to grow physically and spiritually, and to have the abundance of life—a prosperity of friends, of business activities, of health—we must have nourishment.

A plant will die without sunshine or water. It needs to be sustained and maintained. When the land is sour, we use artificial means of fertilizing to sweeten it up. A person without the right vitamins gets beriberi, scurvy, pellagra. And a mind without nourishment sickens and becomes neurotic. But the mind is not poverty-stricken; it has that which can be used. It's a sin to be poor in God's life, it's a sin to be poor in God's body, it's a sin to be poor in God's teaching. That is why we need a firm conviction of the prosperity of living.

God's law says, "If you are aware of Me, I'm aware of you. I'm always here. Turn on to Me." Jesus said, "Come unto me all you who travail and are heavy laden and I will give you comfort." So the potential for greatness resides within each of us and cannot be expressed in our work at home or elsewhere, in our social life, or in our church until we accept its presence. Ernest told me that there are two very important aspects of a gift: the giver and the receiver. God is a willing and generous benefactor; but His gifts of health, prosperity, and peace of mind are lost without our willingness to accept them.

So it's the ability we have that we don't use. To him who hath the flexible mind there's unlimited wealth in all areas. We pray "in the opposite": instead of condemning the existing conditions—for example, making disease a law unto itself—we see and accept the good. Basically, we are always thinking, we are always creating. Constructive thinking expands, blesses, positively affects every area of your life. Destructive thinking decreases, curses, and deteriorates it.

So we might as well begin at some point to choose to think constructively and prosperously and to pray more, to meditate more, and to seek to accept and bless the thing that you think *isn't*—i.e. your good. We need to switch the unhealthy thinking to the healthy thinking. For example: practice thinking what you think God is thinking through you, not what someone has told you you need to think about. Direct the thoughts to the pleasant, loving things. Imagine new experiences, new reactions, new self-images. Limber up the rigidity of the thinking. And, most importantly, "think in the other man's moccasins" —not what someone thinks he is thinking about. Lukewarm water will not take a steam locomotive anywhere. Nor will lukewarm purpose lift us to noticeable heights and achievements.

Ernest Holmes said, "I am grateful for my abundant supply and I give sincere thanks for it. I have decreed it, and it's established under me. I use it freely in the service of God and man, knowing that as it goes out in every way in love and helpfulness to others, it is constantly being blessed, and that further abundance will take its place as fast as it is needed. Now I go out and act accordingly. I express the attitude; I feel and look prosperous; I believe in my prosperity of life—and so I prosper."

Ernest Holmes
Remembered

MY MIND GOES BACK to the beginning, when I first met this man who made such an impact on my life and the lives of countless others. But first I must tell you that I found this teaching in a very strange way. I was groomed, in my childhood religion—the High Episcopal Church, or the Anglican Church if you will—to eventually be an Episcopalian priest. I taught an adult Bible class when I was eleven. I served as an altar boy and a crucifer in the Order of Sir Galahad.

When the Second World War erupted, by a strange fluke I became one of 300 men under 26 that President Roosevelt deferred from the draft. I spent four years setting up war plants, buying matériel for the destruction of other individuals, and I got away from church and teaching and belief. I didn't have much time for it.

After the war, I became an independent industrial engineer —actually an "efficiency expert." But I was still seeking something, and this search led to the establishment of an independent church work, for which I rented the rooftop of the old Hotel Shelburne in New York City; and wherever I was, I flew

97

back in to hold a little service for 15 or 20 people. I had some great people there, but still I wasn't quite happy.

I began to delve into the teachings of the great Truth thinkers of current and past times. I was going through a review of my past life, and like all young red-blooded American boys, I had done some things I wasn't pleased with, and I had paid my price for them. (If you're going to choose to do something, at least take your lumps, pay your price with a smile. The Law is immutable.)

I had never heard of Ernest Holmes when I started reading one of his books. I came to one paragraph that stood out in neon lights: "There is no sin but a mistake. There is no punishment but a consequence." I thought, I have to meet this man!

This, I think, was in 1952. I called to try to get an appointment with Dr. Holmes. To my amazement, I was told I couldn't see him until 1953. I had to wait a year. I thought, This is really something! I'm looking forward to it!

When at last the time came, I booked passage on the Santa Fe Super Chief train because there was an airlines strike. There were some last-minute things I had to do, and when I finished, I found I would be too late for the train. So I booked a place on the next one. That first train went on to become the worst wreck in Union Pacific history. On the next train there were about 30 of us who, let's say, believed enough to take it. There were also almost as many executives of the Union Pacific Railroad running around to make sure we were happy.

I got to Los Angeles and called for a hotel room; but there was none because of the airlines strike. So I hired a cab and drove to Riverside, where I got a room at the old Mission Inn. But I needed to get in to Los Angeles for my daily appointment. There would be about four days of this.

It turned out that there were no taxi cabs, so I made a deal with a helicopter mail pilot—and you have to understand that in those days these gentlemen were truly cowboys right off the ranch. They wore boots. They had medicine under their seat which they freely imbibed of. (I don't know what the medicine was for.) I made a deal where I'd take the morning flight out and the afternoon flight back. One time I asked the pilot, "What happens when that thing up there stops?" He said, "Well, then it's about time for me to have some more medicine. And if you're lucky, you'll get a slug too."

From the helicopter I cabbed in to the Institute of Religious Science at the corner of 6th and New Hampshire, which had been a design studio before being taken over as Religious Science "headquarters." There I met Ernest Holmes and the gentleman who has been a friend and associate ever since—Dr. Bill Hornaday.* I talked to both of them. I was impressed. I was convinced that this was the teaching for me. I decided to have my little Truth group embrace the principles of Ernest Holmes.

Before I left, Bill shook hands with me, and Dr. Holmes patted me on the back and said, "I'm glad you're going to be with us. Build a good work—and don't write home for money." He embraced me.

I went back to New York.

In 1954, the schism that takes place in all religious movements took place in Religious Science, and the Church split into the present United Church structure and the International Association of Religious Science Churches, now Religious Science International. I had studied in New York with Dr. Raymond Charles Barker† and Dr. Paul Martin Brunet. Dr. Barker said,

* William H.D. Hornaday (1910–1992), first pastor of Founder's Church, was Ernest Holmes' most prominent associate and sucessor.

† Raymond Charles Barker (1911–1988) was founder-pastor of New York's First Church of Religious Science and, after Ernest Holmes, the most celebrated speaker and writer in the Religious Science movement.

"George, don't be a traitor; stay with us. We're all staying together."* I shook my head and couldn't understand it. I closed my church and kept the charter and went to Texas, where I pursued my former profession of industrial engineering, acting as a sort of minister-at-large.

I weekly telephoned and spoke to Ernest Holmes. He knew were I was, and I told him what was going on. I was in paradise: the Texas women were beautiful, and I was teaching and lecturing whenever I could. In 1955 I was just settling in, enjoying the Texan life and atmosphere, when I got a call from Ernest. He said, "I need you out here." I packed up and left for Los Angeles.

Once there, I spent a day being interviewed by more dignitaries than I can ever remember, to determine, I guess, whether I was fit. Finally, a little after 5 o'clock, I went into Dr. Holmes' office and I said, "Well, I guess I passed." I remember him saying, "Well, you know, it wouldn't have made any difference what they said anyhow; but we have to go through these processes."

So I was accepted into the official family, with Ernest and Dr. Bill the seniors of all. *I* was sort of low man on the totem pole—learning, and grateful to be around both of them. I was appointed to the ministerial staff of Dr. Hornaday's church. The Headquarters staff at that time was Reginald Armor, Mark Carpenter, Barclay Johnson, William Hornaday, myself, and of course our spiritual leader, Dr. Ernest Holmes.

I found he had a keen insight and a great sense of humor. I buckled down, giving thanks—despite my many youthful mistakes. I soon immersed myself in the life of my new profession. I found my work rewarding and frustrating—because there seemed to be more intrigues than I had experienced in my role

---

* This refers to the group of IARSC ministers who declined to enter into the new organizational arrangements proposed by the Institute of Religious Science, which became the United Church of Religious Science, of which Dr. Bendall remained an adherent, and which Ernest Holmes headed.

of subcontracting during the Second World War in the aircraft and propeller plants.

But I went on.

It's nice to have people tell you you're great. My first sermon to the nice little group I had in New York was apparently a great metaphysical talk. At least nearly everyone said, "Great!" But one old man stopped me at the door and said, "Young man, that's one of the greatest talks about true metaphysics I ever heard."

"Thank you!" I said.

He looked me straight in the eye and said, "But in spite of you, I still believe in God."

Ernest taught me: "Don't look for acclaim." He told me, "George, you are a teacher, as I am. Dr. Hornaday is a minister. Do what you do best: teaching. Be a minister; but be the good teacher I know you have it in you to be."

Ernest was a teacher. He straightened me out one time: He said, "Sure, George, you're a minister and you're a good one; but always remember *the teaching and the practice* is the thing. *Teach* them. That's how you'll minister to them. When you accept that fact within yourself, you'll be a better minister." I've worked at it ever since. *Teach:* because as I teach, I'm giving of myself, I'm touching; I'm blessing and I'm healing; because there's a principle—the principle that Ernest always stood for: Whatever you do, do it knowing you're healing one person.

I counseled with many people, conducted the Wednesday Evening Service (which was known as the suicide service), and enjoyed every minute of it full of vim and vigor. My office at the time had been a storeroom for janitorial supplies, but Augusta Rundel, Hazel Holmes' aunt, had it cleaned up and outfitted with a desk and comfortable chairs. I counseled with all the people that it was impossible for Dr. Holmes and Dr. Hornaday

in their busy schedules to handle. I taught many classes, offi-
ciated at a lot of funerals and weddings.

In this last connection, I remember how on one occasion Dr.
Barclay Johnson, who was head of Affiliated Churches, ran in
to Dr. Holmes and said, "All of Bendall's weddings are invalid!"

Ernest said, "What are you talking about?"

Barclay said, "Well, I didn't hear from him after he left
New York; so I defrocked him and canceled his ministerial
recognition."

Ernest Holmes came out of his seat and said, "Well, he
talked to *me* every week—and I'll give you an hour to re-ordain
him in a proper ceremony!" Everybody scrambled around—and
I was ordained for the second time.

Someone was needed to work in the Black community—Central
Avenue, Adams, and environs. A great many of our members
were residents of that area. At the request of Mabel Gray I was
assigned to that area. I spent two years with great, wonderful,
warm, sensitive people, without whose contribution of time and
money the present church edifice—Founder's—never would
have been realized.

Unrelated to this, but also part of my work, was counseling
people sent to me with an alcoholic problem. However, I was
uninformed and didn't understand this problem. Someone mentioned a group called Alcoholics Anonymous, and I called one
of the people I was counseling and said, "*You've* got to help *me*!
I've got to understand what Alcoholics Anonymous is all about.
Will you take me to some meetings?" So once a week he came
and drove me all around, telling me what a spiritual program it
was. I learned the Twelve Steps, which were the greatest expression of Religious Science in another language that I had ever
seen.

Finally, at a meeting in Puente—typical warehouse, folding
chairs, lights hanging from cords on the ceiling—I found that

strong sense of the higher Power of God. Then I began to understand. I found that with Science of Mind, they could support
their program. Ernest Holmes concurred and encouraged me to
work with them as much as I could—because he was a compassionate man; he loved all kinds of people. Wherever he went, he
was no stranger to anyone.

In 1956 or '57 Dr. Hornaday, in one of his compassionate flashes
of brilliance, brought a professor over from France and established a clinic on Franklin Avenue, where we took mentally
retarded and spastic children rejected by the Tracy Clinic and
worked with them. I spent a year with this. We all made great
sacrifices from our salary, since there was no budget.

We did get a medical officer—Louis Morrow, a prominent
physician—for the clinic. This came about because California
Governor Goodwin Knight, a Religious Scientist and a great
friend of Dr. Holmes, had felt that among the millions of dollars sitting in mental health trust funds some money should be
available to relieve the condition of these children. But we had
to close the clinic at the end of the year—having accomplished
a great deal—because the medical staff sent to inspect it said,
"Well, you did good; but we can't tell whether it's medical or
spiritual-faith healing that's accomplished this; so we're not going to approve it."

After this, Ernest pointed to Santa Monica, where, he said, we
had a great work, one that should not be overlooked. "I think
that would be a good place for you; and then you'll be available
when I need you." So we opened a church in the Santa Monica
Women's Club. I struggled with it, yet it never seemed to grow.
I think I drew $200 a month as reimbursement. Ernest spoke out
there many times, and neither of us could understand why it
didn't "take." Finally, towards the end of one day, as he was ly-
ing on the couch, he looked up at me and said, "You know, I

think I made a mistake: it wasn't Santa Monica I wanted you to go to; it was Venice." I said, "Thanks a lot! *Now* you tell me!" But that, too, was Ernest Holmes.

I was privileged in the last two years of Ernest Holmes' life to live with him. In 1958, after the passing of his wife, Hazel, he came up to my office and said to me, "You lost your first wife and you know what it's like. I don't want to live alone. If you want to, come live with me. The only way I'm going out of this house is feet first."

I moved in for a week, being tested in every way possible. Finally, at the end of the week, Dr. Holmes said, "You've got a lot of love in you; you don't mean to come across as you sometimes do; you can stay." The rules were: "I'm not sitting here for you to alleycat around town; I expect you home every evening. Dinner is at six; if you're not here, you don't eat."

I was given Hazel Holmes' apartment; and so it was Ernest Holmes and myself; Webb, who drove Ernest and who lived in the back; and Lena the cook, who took care of Dr. Holmes. A set of rooms in this vast house were set aside for Adela Rogers St. Johns—so that when she came to town, the three of us could argue beautifully. He always respected Adela.*

One day Adela went to Ernest and asked, "What are you going to do about George Bendall?"

He replied, "What do you mean, what am I going to do?"

She said, "Look at the way he worked and gave of himself."

"What do you want me to do?" he asked.

She said, "Give him a doctorate."

---

* Adela Rogers St. Johns (1894–1988) was a journalist, best-selling author, and popular social historian. She was especially close to Hazel and Ernest Holmes. In common with a number of celebrities, she lent her prestige to the fortunes of the Religious Science movement.

Ernest asked if she would sponsor it, and she said she would. So at the request of Adela Rogers St. Johns, there was conferred on me a doctorate in the Humanities, which at that time was very rare in our movement. I was honored to accept it and went right on with my work.

With my taking up residence in Ernest Holmes' house began some of the most enlightening experiences of my life. We made an agreement that during the day I was Dr. George Bendall of the staff and he was Dr. Ernest Holmes, head of the movement. I never went near him unless he sent his secretary to call me to his office for one reason or another. He told me, "At Headquarters I'm always Dr. Holmes and you must always treat me with respect, but that doesn't apply at home." So the minute I crossed the threshold of that magnificent Tudor mansion at night, those formalities were dropped and I had the freedom to speak as I felt. We talked another language then.

One day I got to the point where I thought I was pretty good—look at all this stuff that I know, I'm a genius at this Science of Mind—and he said, "When you think you know it all, you really don't know anything."

He was a small man; I was 6 feet 3 inches. I would look down on him, but he'd call me "little boy." I guess that was to chop me down to size.

When I was given the privilege of living with Ernest, there were certain ground rules laid down—breakfast at eight, dinner at six; and if you were not on time, you didn't eat. I was not to go out in the evenings without permission unless to teach, because he wasn't going to sit alone in that house. He wasn't bringing me into the house to be out "alleycatting around" (I was single at the time).

Every night we would discuss all of the things that had been on Ernest's mind. For the first few months, I just listened as he talked to me about the principles, his books, what he was going to speak on, soaking it in like a sponge. We talked about treatment, and we treated together every night. It was almost as though he were pounding it all into my head with a hammer—as though he had to get it *all* into *somebody*. I stored it, and even now parts of it are still down in some crevasse of my subconscious.

In order to make sure that he kept on track, I tried to anticipate what he wanted and do it with a smile, although many times in later months, when a physical complaint affected him, he became rather moody. But we managed to stay on the course of Principle.

Every night was a private class—some nights, after he looked at *Maverick* and *Bonanza* (I did have to suffer through those). We'd have dinner, after which Ernest would watch his favorite program, *Bonanza*. Somehow or another he felt the vastness of this thing, the hugeness of the Ponderosa Ranch. Here was all of this loneliness, and these people were coming together and touching other people. This was the thing that appealed to him. There was another one with James Garner in it, a cowboy picture of some kind, and he loved that. He'd sit in his chair with a huge black cigar and watch.

Why we looked at *Maverick* I'll never know. I guess because *he* was a maverick. When that was over, we'd get to work. Then the blessed part—my learning and awareness—began.

Many of the things we did in the evening were focused on a point called mental stretching exercises. There used to be a quote from Romans 12:2 on the wall of the chapel in the old Institute building: "Be not conformed to this world, but be ye transformed by the renewing of your mind." Ernest believed in that. He said, "Otherwise we start conforming to all the ideas that are coming from other people. So we need to keep our minds stretched, limber. It's like a muscle. If you pray a lot, you condition the prayer muscle. If you keep stretching your mind, you allow more into it; you can develop more capacity for the marvelous things you do in your life." He would throw out a point and we would explore it; we'd even take something from one of his books and keep pounding away at it.

Ernest liked to woo his mind. He would be wearing a flannel shirt with big checks and an old sweater when he wasn't at work, and he'd sit there doing these mental gymnastics. I said, "Why do you do that?" and he answered, "That's how I keep in touch with the principles."

He never went to bed at night that he didn't read something. He wore one of those old transparent green bookkeeper's visors. He'd read something, underline it, talk about it, stretch it out. Always stretching his mind.

After all of this kind of thing night after night, I almost felt like a filing cabinet that somebody was storing things away in. I remember talking, and Ernest talking; and I would say, "Why are you doing this?" and he would say, "Well, I told you I wanted you home because I wanted someone to talk with, someone to keep my mind active by contradicting me and arguing with me." But when he prayed or treated, I simply listened.

There were many happy times at that big house at 6th and S. Lorraine, and many people—Goodwin Knight, the Governor; George Lamsa* (he and I got to be friends later; every year until his transition he would come and spend a week, and we'd visit and talk); J. Allen Boone†; Elaine St. Johns; William R.

---

* Assyrian theologian, Aramaic expert, and Bible translator.

† Author of *Kinship of All Life, Letters to Strongheart, The Language of Silence,* etc.

Parker*; Peggy Lee (and I'm still a close friend of Peggy Lee's; she has never taken a platform, gone before a microphone, or cut a record that she hasn't known she is healing somebody. I've always felt she was sort of like a daughter and I was like a son to Dr. Holmes).† Ernest Holmes had this feeling: nobody was a stranger. He always thought that way. He had a great love—love of life and love of others.

A frequent visitor to the house was Fenwicke Holmes, an older brother of Ernest's, who had been an internationally known Congregational minister and author. Ernest was small in stature, but Fenwicke was even smaller. Together they would sit and talk; but it never seemed to go anywhere. Fenwicke had a great ego, and I always felt that he never quite understood his brother, who had never had formal theological training and yet could be the head of a spiritual movement. But they got along. When Fenwicke was going to visit, Ernest would give me money and say, "Go out to dinner. There's no reason for *both* of us to be bored with this."

The two brothers decided one time to write *The Voice Celestial*.‡ Ernest would write things and send them to Fenwicke, and Fenwicke would write things and send them to Ernest. Naturally, Fenwicke seemed to rule the situation. Once, Ernest wrote a poem that he loved. He sent it to Fenwicke, who omitted it from *The Voice Celestial*. Fenwicke for some reason never offered an explanation, except that "it wouldn't fit." So Ernest

* Parker, a professor at Redlands University, and St. Johns (daughter of Adela Rogers St. Johns), a prominent editor and intimate friend of Ernest Holmes, co-authored the best-selling *Prayer Can Change Your Life*, which reported the results of controlled studies of the effectiveness of different kinds of prayer at Redlands University.

† In her autobiography, *Miss Peggy Lee*, the singer gives a warm account of her relationship with Dr. Bendall and Dr. Holmes.

‡ *The Voice Celestial* is "An Epic Poem: Questions All Thoughtful Men Have Asked, Answered by the Wisdom of the Ages." It was published in 1960.

said, "I'm going to read this at the next Tuesday Invitational Meeting." But not too many of the Tuesday group responded enthusiastically. So he gave the original copy to me, saying, "You like it, and I like it; so you can have it."*

From time to time, Ernest would call me into his office, and I would wonder, What did I do now? because I did do quite a few stupid things. He'd say, "Now if you're free . . ." and then he'd say, ". . . I don't want you to get yourself involved if you've made other arrangements. . . ." And I'd say, "Yes, Dr. Holmes," because I knew what was coming.

He'd say to me, "I'm having a small party tonight . . ." and I would brace myself, because that would mean there would be 30 or 40 people. He would say, "Now if it's convenient, I'd like you to be there." Of course, I knew the only answer was yes. And then he'd look at me and say, "You can leave in 15 minutes and start getting things set up." I'd work, work, and be wrung out. After a while I became sort of the assistant host.

He loved to eat; he loved food—even food he shouldn't have eaten. I couldn't eat some of the food he ate. He had a cast iron stomach, coming from New England. When Lena was off, he would make dinner; and why it didn't blow him through the roof I will never understand. He could eat in greasy-spoon kinds of restaurants and digest and enjoy what only a great practitioner could have survived.

I remember that in the last year he decided a little stimulation would be good. His doctor had said it wouldn't hurt, and so he would have me make drinks for those who wished it. I had to go out and buy it, because he had never had a drink in his life (and had never been sick in his life). I came up with something

* The poem, "A Fable," is given in The Philosophy of Ernest Holmes, volume 1 of Dr. Bendall's The Holmes Papers series (Manhattan Beach: South Bay Church of Religious Science, 1989), pp. 234–53.

where I would put about a half-teaspoonful of whiskey in a glass with a lot of grenadine syrup and oranges and fruit—a modified Shirley Temple. And when I'd serve everybody else, I can remember his saying, "Where's *my* cocktail?"

We at Headquarters used to shudder when Ernest would say, "Let's go to Renee's for a hamburger." This was the original Ptomaine Inn of all time, and only Ernest Holmes would be unaffected by anything eaten there. He'd come back from lunch, sit on the steps of the old Institute building in shirtsleeves, shirt open—nobody knew whether he was a bum or a passerby or whatever—and stop people as they walked by and say, "My name's Ernest. What is yours? What do you do?" Whoever he stopped would say, "And what do *you* do?" He'd say, "Oh, I work in there."

This was Ernest Holmes: constantly touching life, touching people. He believed in this interrelationship of life and people.

We'd sit in the lobby at Headquarters, and as you came by: "Who are you?" "How do you feel?" "What did you get out of the class?"

The door to his office was always open. And he had the ability to read you. You could sit down in front of him and he could say, "Ha Ha! This [thing] is your seeming situation; but there's no truth in it. Go and do your thing as you're supposed to and stop worrying about things like that."

That's the kind of individual he was. He loved life to such an extent that he thought that nobody could ever do any wrong.

You must picture what was known as a Tuesday Invitational Meeting—a meeting every Tuesday at which Ernest sat in a chair in front of you, and whatever he felt in his mind he explored. You could attend only by special invitation. People flew in from Phoenix, from Chicago, from Dallas to attend these meetings.

He might even start a Tuesday Meeting out and say, "Now

do you understand this principle of cosmic illumination and how it transforms the particles into ethereal expressions of matter?" And everybody would look and say, "Yes, yes. Absolutely!" And he'd say, "Well, *I* don't." But this was Ernest Holmes. He brought people out of their rigidity. He felt them. He moved into them. He became a part of them. And every word that he spoke became a word that meant something. As he spoke, you translated his words into your own words, because the truth was caught and you felt it and translated it at your level.

Following Ernest's talk we would go downstairs and eat a brown-bag lunch. Being thrifty at the time, I never made a brown-bag lunch, because there were enough people down there who always had something left over that I could eat. I think that I was the only minister in attendance at those Invitational Meetings, and I used to sit at the back of the room enthralled by the continuous flow of spontaneous ideas. I made many notes of the talks. Ernest would send me copies of them afterwards, because they were tape-recorded. And I thought, What a tragedy that the world isn't exposed to the wisdom shared at these sessions.

Ernest Holmes didn't like barriers between himself and people. In fact, most of the time when he counseled with you, he moved from behind the desk and sat down in a chair beside you. When he spoke, he didn't like flowers or people cluttering up the platform, because he liked to be free with the people.

But he had fun. Once, he said in a loud whisper, "Look how pious they all are! Look at their faces! I'll take care of that." So he jumped up and I introduced him. He talked for a few minutes and then went into the biggest pile of gibberish that I have ever heard. Then he stopped and asked, "Do you all agree with what I've just said?"

They all said, "Oh, yes!"

He shook his head and looked out and said, "Well, I didn't agree with a word of it." Then they all laughed.

That was Ernest Holmes. *Live it, practice it, and express it.*
He never forced. He didn't manipulate life; he flowed with it.

To illustrate the kind of man he was: I remember how, when
we were at the Wiltern Theater—Reg Armor,* Bill Hornaday,
myself, and Ernest Holmes—every once in a while you'd have
no feeling for what the soloist was singing about, they were so
carried away with their vocal technique or whatever. And Ernest
would say in his loud stage-whisper, "Why do they all sing about
things they don't understand?" This would fracture the poor
singer. Afterwards he would take the soloist by the hand and
smile and say, "I love you; you know it" and completely dis-
solve whoever it was—because this was Ernest Holmes. This
was the feeling. Behind all the pixieness was always that feeling that he touched you; and as he touched you, you were being healed, you were being restored.

As I was with him longer, I began to freely express what I
felt. And I remember one time, while Dr. Hornaday was away—
probably in Africa with Albert Schweitzer—I was with Dr.
Holmes at the Wiltern when he gave a talk. Afterwards, he asked
me how I liked it. I said, "Where *were* you? You didn't make any
sense. You were all over the place. Anybody who could follow
you had to be crazy." I asked him, "Ernest, why don't you talk
about the points you tell me you're going to talk about?" He
said, "OK, I'll talk to *you*; you write the points down; and I'll
have them in front of me when I speak."

The next Sunday, the four points he said he was going to talk
about I put on a piece of paper, which I left on the lectern at the
Wiltern. He came out and looked down at this piece of paper—I
don't think he ever expected me to do it. Then he held the paper
up and waved it around and said, "Look! George thinks I ought

* Reginald Armor (1903–1977) was still in his teens when he associated
himself with Ernest Holmes and the Religious Science teaching, which he
served by Holmes' side for the rest of his life.

to talk to you about *this.*" And he kept grinding it in. "George wrote this down, so I'm going to talk about it." He had a lot of fun with it. (I felt very embarrassed.)

The following Sunday, I didn't put any paper there. So he turned around and said, "Where is my outline?"

This is the kind of relationship we had.

During the time that I was in Santa Monica, like a lot of people I was often short of funds. Ernest had the healthiest concept about money of all the people I've ever known. He would sense my shortage, and when I came down for breakfast and picked up my napkin there would be a hundred-dollar bill by my plate— because he couldn't stand for the people in his house to be without money. In fact, when Founder's Church was being built, a certain sum of money was needed, and Ernest sat down that night and said, "I'm going to treat. I need $180,000 by the end of the week, and I am going to treat for it."

"Why don't you treat for *more?*" I asked.

He said, "I only need $180,000 at the moment; and I want you to join me in this treatment."

"I don't know how to treat like that," I replied. "I'll treat that *more than enough* to meet your needs is there."

He said, "I'll show you a check before the end of the week."

At the end of the week, he had a check for $180,000.

I was in awe.

He had absolutely no sense of limitation about money. He shared with me that many times in the early days he traveled around the country, tacked up a sign: "ERNEST HOLMES SPEAKS TONIGHT," collected the money, stuffed it in a suitcase, and came back from the trip sometimes with as much as $10,000. The miracle to me is that nobody ever hit him over the head and took it. But then, he had a wonderful sense of protection and of his own worth, and a magnificent sense of unlimited abundance, health, and money.

I can remember him at the ministerial conferences, as he walked through the grounds in a checkered shirt and brown sweater, smoking one of his famous cigars. He might say, "Now I want all the ministers to be permissive. I want them to do whatever they want to do." And then I can remember him sitting in his chair and looking up, saying, "Where's Barclay Johnson! Why isn't he here yet?"

He made a mental check, and when all of his protégés were present, he would get up and say, "You see: we're all part of each other."

Which was true. It became a part of us that everyone everywhere in every Religious Science church was a part of the other one. We weren't separate churches. We weren't separate people. We were all one in unity in one expression.

Ernest touched you. Once you were exposed to him, it was as though you were touched by a flame of light. You were inspired. You were lifted up. You wanted *to do something.*

He said, and many will remember this, that when they threw Daniel into the den with the lions, it wasn't that Daniel wasn't afraid of the lions. It was that Daniel had so much *love* that the lions were not afraid of him. Ernest said that love was the lodestone of all life. That was Ernest Holmes: always one who touched you; always one who wasn't afraid to take the biggest man in the world and embrace him.

Ernest taught me always to touch people when entering a building. And that was to just basically, within yourself, with your eyes closed or open, imagine your arms growing and growing and finally embracing the entire building. The love that you have to give then touches that building and everyone in it. This is the way Ernest always entered a building.

You never take a platform and never speak unless the love within you reaches out to everybody in that room. And you always get it back. I've learned it. For the only healing agent is love. No healings, no great works take place without that true emotion of love.

Ernest Holmes was always growing. He was always human. He was always feeling things. What many people forget who think only of the Law and the Principle of Science of Mind is the great feeling and the great ability to touch humanity at all levels. He touched with the mind, he touched with the voice, he touched with the heart. He touched in every way that he could think of. Wherever he walked, a radiance went out from him.

This is the Ernest Holmes that lives in our hearts. This is the Ernest Holmes that insinuates itself into every line of our teaching—not just the fact that there is a Law of Cause and Effect; not just the fact that there's a law that responds with mechanical regularity to the spontaneity of your thoughts. Not just this, but a deep sense of awareness, of people, of feeling, of touch. Wherever Ernest Holmes went, he touched people.

We talk about Law and Principle to such an extent that we sometimes make the greatest teaching in the world a mathematical formula—and it isn't. I found that in the past few years we had gotten to a point where we had overlooked the feeling. We had not only thrown the baby out with the wash water, we were throwing the baby's father out too. And I'm so glad to see the living spirit of Ernest Holmes returning to prominence.

This is the feeling. This is the sense of touch that I am happy to see being restored, revitalized, re-expressed in the framework of our teaching. This is the feeling that can establish what Ernest Holmes wanted: a group of people that could practice what is inside the Science of Mind textbook.

On that memorable night of February 12, 1959—the occasion of Dr. Holmes' Cosmic Consciousness experience—he touched every soul gathered for the dedication of Christ Church of Religious Science at Whittier. This was a genuine mystical experience.

Previously he had written that mystics are those who have been illumined. They have all had an experience in common: they have seen the Cosmic Light. Emerson walking across Boston Common, Thoreau in Concord, suddenly became conscious of it. Edward Carpenter walked a bridge and thought all of New York City was afire. Mystics have all seen this light and have never been the same afterwards; but they've been perfectly normal human beings. But, he says, we find that people who spend a great deal of time in prayer, meditation, or communion gradually take on a new atmosphere, a new sweetness, a light that all people sense. Some people even have the ability to see a person's aura, a light enveloping the body. And then, he adds, it seems that in all forms of healing, all that can be done is to let an inner light flow to restore us to our original pattern of perfection. And he follows that with this last line: We need to break through our habitual thought patterns, which repeat themselves with monotonous regularity.*

Let me briefly relate something of the occasion and circumstances of the experience that Ernest had in 1959, when Cosmic Consciousness became so much a part of him, and then tell how he prepared for this experience during the time I was with him.

In his address to the Whittier congregation, he observes that our movement is growing and expanding very rapidly—"as rapidly, I think, as is possible—because we wouldn't wish to mistake its end and purpose, which is not the building of churches. It is not the dedicating of churches. It's what happens in them after they are built." It's what happens whenever a group of people with our conviction meet together "for the only two purposes for which we exist—teaching and practice." We are a teaching and practicing order in the Christian Faith that

---

* See Holmes' *The Science of Mind*, pp. 343–46, and "The Healing Light," in *The Anatomy of Healing Prayer*, volume 2 of Dr. Bendall's *The Holmes Papers* series (Marina del Rey, Calif.: De Vorss & Co., 1991), pp. 23–40.

believes in two great realities: the Divine Presence and a Power for good. And then he says that it's not our endeavor to convert anybody to our faith. "It's to *prove* something—first of all to ourselves; then to the world. . . ."

The only authority that we have is the authority of "the work that follows the word." He says, "We are a teaching order, not a preaching order . . . [but] we have not yet done what I believe we should do with our membership." Now we're here, he says, to dedicate a church, a physical building. But *it's* here because the consciousness of the people is here. And towards the end of his talk, very briefly he says, "And I see you uniting in one great hymn of praise, one great union of effort, one crescendo of song, and one enveloping light of consciousness . . ." and after a 12-second pause: "I see it!" in a hushed but dynamic voice. A 10-second pause, and then: "Oh God . . ." and then a 5-second pause, after which: "The veil is thin between." After a pause he says, "We do . . . mingle with the host of heaven." Then another pause, and "I see it. And I shall speak no more."*

I can remember the aftermath of this experience. He sat in a chair, Buddha-fashion, with his legs crossed under him. He was smoking a foul-smelling cigar—typically Ernest Holmes. (I used at times to find it difficult to reject the offer of a cigar, but I did.) When I came in, we sat alone in his huge (20 feet by 36, with a 14-foot ceiling) living room, and I said, "You had it, didn't you!"

"You must never tell anyone," he said; "because people won't believe it. They wouldn't know what it was."

---

* The wholly accurate transcript of Dr. Holmes' address to the Whittier congregation, punctuated—and terminated—by this most unexpected and deeply moving experience (to speaker and audience alike), together with an account of the occasion and its aftermath, is given in *The Anatomy of Healing Prayer*, volume 2 of Dr. Bendall's *The Holmes Papers* series (Marina del Rey, Calif.: DeVorss & Co., 1991) pp. 129–36.

"What happened?" I asked.

He said, "While I was talking, it seemed as though every-thing turned into shimmering waves of light, and I imagined my-self severed from my body, up above and looking down at myself talking, and feeling this thing. People will never believe this; so you can't talk about it."

Indeed, later on, when his biography was being written by his brother Fenwicke, I told Fenwicke that I would be very happy to share these matters with him and that he could do with them what he wanted. Still later, Fenwicke told me that the pub-lishers and the Church review board felt that the matter should not be discussed, because nobody would believe it.*

We went on and, as I looked at him, I noticed things that I

---

* Fenwicke Holmes' biography of his brother discusses Dr. Holmes' reflec-tions on mysticism toward the close of his life. Yet it is strikingly silent about the Cosmic Consciousness experience—possibly in deference to Dr. Holmes' own wishes. However Dr. Bendall has privately suggested that there were other portions of the story of Dr. Holmes' last years that were deleted from the biography before publication. He attributed this to church politics, one signifi-cant element of which was his own ostracism by the powers that succeeded Dr. Holmes in the church administration. One high-ranking veteran of this period today states emphatically that there was very real jealousy of Dr. Holmes' fondness for Dr. Bendall as well as resentment of the close relation-ship the latter enjoyed with the founder and head of the Church of Religious Science. Perhaps not so strangely, then, the biography nowhere makes men-tion of Dr. Bendall, despite his unique relationship with Dr. Holmes.

Silence on the Cosmic Consciousness experience was broken in 1971 with the publication of a somewhat abridged and flawed transcript of the occasion as taped at the Whittier church dedication. A brief introduction mentions that Holmes later spoke of his experience to "a friend." Sixteen years later, Elaine St. Johns, who knew Dr. Holmes and Dr. Bendall intimately, restored some balance to the record in an article appearing in the Dec. 1987 issue of *Science of Mind* magazine. She refers to Dr. Bendall as "very important to Ernest in his last lonely years." Referring to the Cosmic Consciousness experience, she adds: "And he is important to this story too, for . . . George Bendall was the only individual with whom he ever discussed it." Bendall, she tells us, had be-come "instant 'family' " to Dr. Holmes at the very outset of the two years that they lived under the same roof.

had read in Maurice Bucke's *Cosmic Consciousness*, about "the great illumined of all times in cosmic consciousness expressed." I noticed a great radiance, almost a cherubic quality in his countenance. As it was, he often looked like a cherub. Ernest was a small man, but you had no concept of his short stature, because his magnetic personality always touched you; he always had a radiant look. This night, he was even more radiant. He was bathed in an emotion of joy.

He had had an illumination. He said, "I actually had the feeling that I was part of the stars, that I was part of everything, that I was part of the whole movement, the push and pull, of the whole universe"; and he added, "I thought I had had Cosmic Consciousness experiences long before this, but now I know this is truly what it is." Ernest had never been afraid of death, but now there was a complete and total recognition of nothing but eternal life, and he could say, "I'm ready to go anytime now." There was no sense of any mistakes in his life; there was only an instantaneous recognition of his experience and expression as an individual. All of these things I had found in Bucke's *Cosmic Consciousness*. And I thought, Truly I have lived to see just such an individual—as did the 400 people in the Whittier Church who experienced it and were touched by it.

But now let's go back. Ernest had, in a sense, prepared for this; he had prepared for it all his life by his teaching, by his touch with people—because there has never been anything unusual about anyone who has had a Cosmic Consciousness experience. He'd been preparing for it especially with his "experiments." He'd been working with the idea that Light was the perfect energy; that with Light itself—an inner illumination within his meditation and treatment—the transcendence that he believed in could be achieved. So there had been preparation for this Cosmic Consciousness experience of his with a unique set of experiments.

It was a time when I was still on Dr. Hornaday's staff at Headquarters and I remember going home one evening. Always when I got home, Ernest would have been there an hour before. He was in the den, sitting in his favorite little stuffed leather chair, when I walked in the door, and it was not "Hi, George. Dinner is ready. You're late." Instead it was "Did you know that prayer is an energy?"

I said, "What are you talking about? Sure it's an energy."

"How do you know that?" he asked, and I said, "Because all thought is motion; thought is spontaneous; and prayer is nothing but a spontaneous verbalizing of my thought. So it has to be an energy."

"What does an energy have?" he asked, and I said, "An energy has vibrations, and whenever there are vibrations there is sound." (You see, the marvelous thing is that one's whole personality can project itself in an entirely different direction from today forward. You can walk out of here with your mental vibrations going before you, transforming your pathway, transforming your life, because one attitude changed affects the vibration.)

He asked, "Do you think that applies to our work?"

"Certainly," I said.

"Let's try an experiment," he suggested. "Where did I pray?"

In his deep meditative presence we stumbled on it one day. I walked to a chair and I said, "You treated here."

"Yes, I did; but how do you know?"

I said, "I feel something and I don't know what it is."

So we played with this for a couple of months. Then he said, "We must experiment with this a great deal more, because prayer *is* an energy, a movement in mind; prayer is something that reorganizes the creative process and principle into our desire. And wherever there's motion, there could possibly be sound."

So we kept working on it all over that vast house—in the patio, wherever—and towards the end we could in nine cases out of ten, by feeling, become aware of the place where Ernest Holmes prayed. He was building to this experience of Cosmic Consciousness.

I walked around and there seemed to be one particular spot where there was a *sound*—something very much like the sound you get when a group of people such as ours goes into a deep silence in a communion of prayer. More prosaically, it was like a hum, the same kind of hum as when you put a seashell to your ear.

I said, "You prayed *there*." And that's where it was.

So night after night Ernest and I tried these experiments in treatment and prayer. He would pray and treat all over the house—you've got to try to picture this twenty-three room house with a huge patio and a garage (and what they used to call a garage, I would like to live in)—and all over the grounds; and it became a sort of game for me to come home and guess where he had prayed and meditated and treated. Contrary to the popular scoffing at the time, I found that I could do it 90 percent of the time. There's a vibration, an energy—because all thought is in motion. I could feel that vibration. We worked on it and became very good at it. Ernest said, "These are the kind of things we need to build."

I remember one night a friend from the Santa Monica church had a massive heart attack and they brought him to the hospital where he was placed in a room near the morgue because they didn't want to disturb the other patients when he made his transition. (A very thoughtful hospital.) I went home to Ernest wringing my hands. We sat down, and I learned something.

He said, "Now we are going to start with the idea that we are not going to keep this man alive; we haven't got that power. But what we're going to do is work on the idea that the Spirit of God within him expresses Itself to the highest and fullest degree; and we'll let him choose whether he stays or goes. We'll turn him into Light and see what happens." That seemed very cold to me at the time. Finally we prayed.

At eleven o'clock I was still sitting there, working at it like grinding coffee beans. He got up and said, "Good night. I'll see you in the morning."

I thought, How can he do this? I sat up all night, praying, treating, talking to God, screaming at God. I'd look up and say, "Why me, God?" and that "voice" would come down, "Why *not* you?" Finally, at about five o'clock in the morning, exhausted, I felt something.

Later that morning, blue eyes flashing, bright and chipper, Ernest asked, "Well, did you have a good night, George?"

I growled at him and said, "Well, I finally got the treatment through; and I felt good about it."

"Well, I knew the same," he said; "that's why I went to bed last night." And here I had been forcing, deep down trying to manipulate something, and now realizing that I knew nothing about prayer or treatment. So I went to the hospital, and there the man was, on the edge of the bed screaming for orange juice. He lived another ten years. Later, his wife wrote a note saying that he was resigning from the church because Silent Unity had answered her prayers. They were going to join the Unity church.

Ernest taught me something there too. He said, "Never hold on to anybody. When an experience is over, know that you've given what you had to to that experience. Then release them to move on in growth."

I remember one morning we were talking, and he took a salt shaker, picked it up, and moved it. And he asked, "What did I just do?"

"You moved the salt shaker. Why didn't you ask me to pass it to you?" I asked.

"No," he said; "stop kidding. There's a very definite principle involved. How many people does it take to pick up this salt shaker and move it and convince gravity to hold it in its new place?"

"Naturally," I replied, "it takes only one."

"How many people does it take to have a prayer answered, an affirmation accepted, or to make a treatment effective?"

"One."

"That," he said, "is what we have to know: one with God is a majority. It takes only one to know. It only takes one here this morning to know the healing truth. It takes only one to be convinced of a restoring, renewing, revitalizing expression—and that is the Spirit, the Christos within us."

Another time he said, "Do you see that salt shaker?"

"Yes."

"What holds it there?"

"Gravity."

"Now pick it up and move it." I picked it up and moved it.

"Now," he said, "what did you do?"

"Well, I picked it up and I moved it."

"How did you know that it would stay there when you put it down?"

"Because gravity holds it."

"That's what I mean," he said. "The principles never fail. The principles: whenever you're mixed up, go back to the principles."

Ernest more than once told me: "The principles will never let you down. People may. But if you find that people let you down, then you weren't listening when the principles were being taught you. *Thou shalt have no other gods before me.*"

Ernest Holmes loved the Science of Mind teaching, never deviated from it, and always stayed on Principle. You hear all of us who knew him and worked with him say he gave the world the greatest teaching it has ever known—the only teaching that contains no doctrine, tenets, dogma, superstition, or fear.

He had a favorite expression: "Don't throw the baby out with the wash water." And he always said to be careful in extracting techniques and principles that you don't let go that which makes the rose smell sweet.

He said to me, "The greatest single thing we have to get rid of is the idea of judgment. We set up so many judgments, so many different moral codes." And he said, "Our teaching has no doctrine. Our teaching has no tenets. Our teaching has no dogma. Our teaching is the only teaching in the world free of fear and superstition and ignorance. It has none of these things; and until we arrive at this point of understanding, we shall be just as clods plodding around the face of the earth."

He saw the God, the Perfection, within, and it was part of his teaching. He said something that I have never forgotten: "Our teaching prepares us to live today, not to die tomorrow. Because if we live today to the fullest, accepting the gift of life, then our life is eternal in an eternal continuity of expression."

I said to him once, "You know, this teaching is extremely difficult."

He said, "Why?"

I said, "Because it's so simple. It takes away all of my pet things. I can't be guilty. I can't feel rejected, because the only way I can be rejected is if I reject myself. I can't even enjoy playing good old-fashioned sin anymore. You taught me it's a missing of the mark. I can't have anxiety and fears about what is going to happen. The teaching is too simple. I was brought up to deliciously enjoy all these things, then go talk to a priest and get absolution."

Someone asked Ernest, "How do you define what you people stand for?" He was asked this on a national television show with twelve or thirteen clergymen—I guess members of the National Council of Churches. And he said, "We are Judeo-Christian practical transcendentalists." This, of course, stopped the Council members dead in their tracks. Because there is no argument with such a statement. And it is true; this *is* what we are.

Ernest loved honesty. He said that our teaching is one of honesty, and that when we mask it with a lot of mumbo-jumbo, we lose that honesty and lose the ability to heal. He told me that there had been a great practitioner, Ivy Crane Shelhamer. "Years ago, everybody told me I shouldn't have her because she didn't speak perfectly correct English. But every Sunday night at her meeting the halls of Headquarters were filled, and people were walking out healed." And he said, "This is the important thing —the touch; what they feel; not the correctness of the English word."

Ernest once said, "Here we are a group of people who certainly ought to be very happy that we know something; but we ought to be very sad that we aren't doing more about it. We have a knowledge, we have a technique; but I wonder if we have a timidity about it." Ernest believed in courting the Divine Presence and experiencing centeredness—not in abstract or far-off ways. The Divine Presence was there when he broke bread with you, and the Divine Presence was there when he was kidding you. The Divine Presence was there even when he was correcting you for some of the things you should have done and hadn't done.

I asked him once, "Ernest, what's the trouble with the world?" He answered by saying, "Back of it all, they're so lonely, with such a sense of frustration and isolation, that with it comes an unconscious sense of guilt and rejection." He wanted us to stop compartmentalizing ourselves. He wanted us to be united in one humanity.

Ernest had a great love for the churches, or, as we label them, "the field." The movement originally was a group of independent churches with their autonomy, yet affiliated, together with a common dedication to the teaching and practice, and a common response to the loving leadership of Dr. Ernest Holmes. Whenever and wherever he could, he visited the field, lectured in the field. He encouraged me to do the same thing, for he felt that the strength of the entire thing was based on the unity of his field churches. In fact he would send me out sometimes when there was a problem in the field to try and work it out. Sometimes we'd work it out in King Solomon fashion; but always the field was united. There were many bickerings and petty arguments; yet a great unity of purpose bound us all together. His goal was that the field churches would each be a center for healing, speaking the truth and touching people from all walks of life.

I can't recall how many times when a field church was in trouble, Ernest Holmes would write them a check from his own funds so that their temporary problem could be alleviated. He told me one time that if he had it to do over, he would follow the Mormon pattern and never allow a church to exceed 500 members. He felt that the bigger the church, the more personal contact was sacrificed by each individual member. He conveyed to me that the one thing he was concerned about was what would eventually happen to the field. He tried unsuccessfully to have separate funds for field development, field expansion. He tried to get the field to express their opinions. And in every way he could, he worked with them and helped them. He was a counselor and "father confessor" to many of the field ministers. He helped many with their own problems; and of course there are many that he helped in their ministerial success. Oh so many of them.

He said, "You know, we can train ministers as beautifully as we're doing—we have the finest training for ministers in the world—but you can't tell anything about them until we put them in a pulpit and see how they touch the people out in front of them. Whether a minister is an evangelist preaching Christ and him crucified or whether he's a Buddhist or Hindu, it doesn't matter. The only thing that he can deliver to anybody is to give that person back to himself, and with it a sense of security in the Universe in which he lives—*without fear.*"

When I was living with Ernest, he said, "George, one of our biggest problems is that we worship false gods: we worship people, places, and things—effects. That is what is bothering me a little with this building."*

I asked him, "Did you see the picture Dr. Bill has?† Bill doesn't care about any of this; he's treating away. He has a watercolor drawing of what the building is going to look like. He has it propped up in his office and is showing it to everybody."

Ernest struggled for a month. Then he said "I'm going to support it one million percent." I asked why.

"Well," he said, "I look at it as more than a structure. Through me, through Dr. Bill and all the others, the teaching is a covenant and it needs an ark; and so I see this building as symbolic of the ark—and the covenant is the teaching and practice, and I know they will be safe there." So he threw himself into the building campaign totally and completely.

Ernest had always felt hurt that Dr. Frederick Bailes had left the movement and started an independent work, calling it the Science of Mind Church. One time after many years Fred Bailes called and said, "Ernest, I want to come back into the movement." I have a suspicious nature, so I wondered why he wanted to come back at this late date.

A few days later Ernest announced to me very proudly, "I got

---

* Founder's Church of Religious Science.

† William H. D. Hornaday is generally considered the prime mover of the Founder's building campaign and was its pastor from 1960 to his passing in 1992.

Dr. Fred Bailes back in the movement. He's going to retire and I'm going to appoint a minister in his place."

I asked how he got him back. He said, "Well, it really wasn't too much; all Fred wanted was to be reimbursed for the *Home Study Course** that he had paid for, copies of which he still had on hand."

"What did you give him for it?" I asked.

"Well," he said, "the Board wouldn't give the money, so I wrote a check for it myself."

"How much?"

"Eighteen thousand dollars."

I've always thought to myself Bailes had the last laugh. He retired with $18,000 of Ernest Holmes' money.

I said to him one night, "Ernest, you have always been known as what is a pot-stirrer. You tell everybody that they're going to be head of the movement someday and you like to pit them all against each other. That's an old Boston, New England type of operation. That's fine; but basically I feel your subconscious attitude is that you created this thing, and if you can't take it with you, nobody is going to have it. And so you've set it up so that there is no provision for a successor or a leader."

He didn't speak to me for three days.

At the end of the three days he said, "You know, I think you're probably right. As soon as I get to feeling better, I've got to do something about it. There are a few people I need to talk to."

I said, "While you're at it, why don't you write a white paper —something about what you see for the movement down the road?" He replied, "I'm not imposing my will on anybody. Let them figure it out for themselves."

---

* Published today as *Basic Principles of the Science of Mind.*

One of the things Ernest always wanted was a unification of the two organizations.* He called them spoiled brats. He used to lecture for both; often, too, he went in the summer to Lee's Summit, Missouri, and lectured there for the Unity people.

Ernest arranged for Adela Rogers St. Johns, who stayed at the house whenever she was in Los Angeles (she had her own suite of rooms), to mediate a preliminary set of unification talks that he had scheduled for the summer of 1960. Dr. Raymond Charles Barker and Dr. Robert H. Bitzer would represent the IARSC.† For our side, there would be Dr. Holmes—and myself, in as much as Dr. Barker had known me, and I had always been interested in the field.

Ernest very much looked forward to these talks. He had told Raymond Barker, "If anything happens to me, George knows what I want. He'll go on with the talks." He discussed this with certain members of the Board, and they concurred.

After Ernest's transition in April 1960, Adela called me to say that Dr. Barker was willing to go on with the talks. I had to ask to get back to her, because now I had to go through a bureaucracy of boards and committees—very different from when I was living with Ernest: he'd tell me what he wanted, and I would go out and say, "This is what Dr. Holmes wants." This time I had to get the permission of a national board.

The message came back to me: Mind your own business. So I dropped it.

---

* This refers to the two major organizations within Religious Science, today known as *United Church of Religious Science* and *Religious Science International*, each with its own headquarters, member churches, and groups. All of Dr. Bendall's references to church, headquarters, etc., are to the former organization.

† International Association of Religious Science Churches—the present-day Religious Science International. Dr. Bitzer opened the first Religious Science branch work, the Hollywood Church of Religious Science.

We're still trying to find a way to unite the two organizations. Ernest always felt it was a split in the mind of man, but
not in the mind of God.

Ernest often confided in me the moods of depression that he
masked from the world. As soon as Dr. Hornaday's church was
finished, his own work would be done. He wanted to see that
completed.* He wanted to be with his wife of many years,
Hazel. Much of his life had seemingly departed with her.†

I tried to lift his spirits and get him to understand that we
all needed him. I gathered that he was emotionally tired. He felt
that his work was just about completed. He often said that he
had made many mistakes, and he wondered what might have
happened with the movement if he had been of a different temperament.‡

We talked at great length about many things, because by this
time we shared a closeness of understanding. A subtle change
had taken place. I confess I think I had gone there seeking a
father, but after a while—especially in the last months, with
Ernest's illness—I found that I was becoming something of a
father-confessor to Ernest Holmes.

We talked a great deal, about two months before he had a
stroke, before his transition. He said, "George, I want to tell you
something. You know I'm going to be leaving soon—and I want
to. I miss Hazel. I've done the things I set out to do. The church
is being built. I've got almost everything taken care of."

Then he said, "George, if anything happens to me, you con-

---

* Ground was broken for Founder's Church in 1958, and the edifice was
dedicated, with Dr. Holmes himself presiding, less than two years later, in
January of 1960.

† Hazel Holmes had passed away in 1957.

‡ In private conversation, Dr. Bendall said that this had particularly to do
with Dr. Holmes' judgment in regard to certain personages in the movement.

tinue to keep your interest in the field. There are beautiful people out there, and I think that a good work for you would be a kind of field liaison, because you love the field and the field loves you. In this way we can keep the continuity of the whole thing going." But through some chain of circumstances, this never seemed to develop or work out.

He said, "I want you to remember something: when I pass on, if anyone comes by and tells you that they have talked with me, you tell them they're nuts. Because," he said, "I've got work to do; I'm going down the line. I'm not looking back over my shoulder."*

I've always felt that during the last year, he could have healed his sickness, but he didn't want to. He wanted to go. Two weeks before the final transition, Ernest Holmes had a stroke. He could not talk. It was a rather shocking blow. I had begun to think of him as immortal and eternal.

There was much business at the house. His physician, Dr. Omar Fareed, couldn't have been more attentive and loving. A special nurse was hired for him. I can remember that the nurse would sometimes come to me and say, "I think he wants you." I said, "Wants me? He can't even talk!" She would say, "Just go in." I would sit there, and somehow mentally, with tremendous concentration, I would ask questions and get answers by working with the affirmative side of the feelings exchanged in mind. I'm sure that even to this day, some people (myself included) think I imagined it all. Yet as I recall it now, it was very real.

I came home one time and found a line of people in the hall-way; and I said to Lena, "What's going on here?!" She said, "I let them in: they're all going in to kneel by Dr. Holmes' bed and

---

* Notwithstanding this, there was published in 1974 an account purporting to be of Ernest Holmes' messages from "other dimensions."

pray for him." (I've suspected that Lena was taking a tip from each one to allow them to go in and pray; however I had nothing to really justify my feelings). I thought, After all, he's got the power of choice; mightn't this just possibly be the greatest act of malpractice ever perpetrated in the annals of prayer for others—? Because here many, many people were kneeling and praying—which could only have troubled him—to overcome something that, when you came right down to it, was in Ernest Holmes' and God's hands.

The night of Ernest's transition, just before he left us, it seemed he was saying, "Why? why? why?"

I remember the memorial service at Founder's Church. For some reason, they didn't feel I should participate in the service. I was offered a seat in the Family Room, but I preferred to sit out with the people—because that is what Ernest Holmes was, a man of the people.

I guess it was five weeks I sat alone in that house after Ernest's transition. It was a very creepy feeling, sitting in a huge 23-room brick house by yourself day in and day out. I was something of a custodian until the estate got sorted out.

There was a knock on the door, the bell rang, the door was heavily knocked again. I opened it, and a woman stood there saying, "I have a message from Ernest Holmes."

In sort of a trance-like disbelief I looked at her and said, "No thank you, he's not here," and shut the door.

But the feeling of Ernest Holmes, the awareness, is not that he is dead. The feeling is that he lives in our hearts and minds. And even if the name *Science of Mind* departs the scene, never can his teaching perish.

George P. Bendall, L.H.D.

"Nothing is so strong as gentleness, nothing so gentle as real strength," said St. Francis DeSales. This can be said of Dr. George Bendall. His strength, his kindness, his sincerity, and his love and devotion to the purity of the teaching of Dr. Ernest Holmes will live on and on.

He has moved onward and upward into a new life, taking a "little bit" of us with him and leaving a "little bit" of himself behind. What he left behind is like a shining star—a symbol of the faith, the kindness, and the dignity he represented. He will be missed but not forgotten. Truly Dr. Bendall found the Kingdom, for the peace, serenity, and understanding love he radiated came from within. What a privilege indeed to have known him and to have loved him! He will live in my heart for ever.

Ann C. Bendall